Christmas card address book

Keep Track Books

This Christmas card address book helps you keep your Christmas card addresses in one place and track when you send and receive cards.

The book is organized alphabetically with 6 pages for each letter of the alphabet. In addition to having space for addresses and emails, each address box contains a tracker for sent and received cards.

To use the tracker
* fill in the year box '20__' with the current year
* tick the 'S' (=Sent) box when you send a card
* tick the 'R' (=Received) box when you receive a card

Have a wonderful Christmas!

CreateSpace, Charleston SC
Design © Keep Track Books

Name										
Address	20__		20__		20__		20__		20__	
	S	R	S	R	S	R	S	R	S	R
	20__		20__		20__		20__		20__	
Email	S	R	S	R	S	R	S	R	S	R

Name										
Address	20__		20__		20__		20__		20__	
	S	R	S	R	S	R	S	R	S	R
	20__		20__		20__		20__		20__	
Email	S	R	S	R	S	R	S	R	S	R

Name										
Address	20__		20__		20__		20__		20__	
	S	R	S	R	S	R	S	R	S	R
	20__		20__		20__		20__		20__	
Email	S	R	S	R	S	R	S	R	S	R

Name										
Address	20__		20__		20__		20__		20__	
	S	R	S	R	S	R	S	R	S	R
	20__		20__		20__		20__		20__	
Email	S	R	S	R	S	R	S	R	S	R

A

Name											

Address	20__		20__		20__		20__		20__	
	S	R	S	R	S	R	S	R	S	R

	20__		20__		20__		20__		20__	
Email	S	R	S	R	S	R	S	R	S	R

Name											

Address	20__		20__		20__		20__		20__	
	S	R	S	R	S	R	S	R	S	R

	20__		20__		20__		20__		20__	
Email	S	R	S	R	S	R	S	R	S	R

Name											

Address	20__		20__		20__		20__		20__	
	S	R	S	R	S	R	S	R	S	R

	20__		20__		20__		20__		20__	
Email	S	R	S	R	S	R	S	R	S	R

Name											

Address	20__		20__		20__		20__		20__	
	S	R	S	R	S	R	S	R	S	R

	20__		20__		20__		20__		20__	
Email	S	R	S	R	S	R	S	R	S	R

A

Name

Address

20__		20__		20__		20__		20__	
S	R	S	R	S	R	S	R	S	R

20__		20__		20__		20__		20__	
S	R	S	R	S	R	S	R	S	R

Email

Name

Address

20__		20__		20__		20__		20__	
S	R	S	R	S	R	S	R	S	R

20__		20__		20__		20__		20__	
S	R	S	R	S	R	S	R	S	R

Email

Name

Address

20__		20__		20__		20__		20__	
S	R	S	R	S	R	S	R	S	R

20__		20__		20__		20__		20__	
S	R	S	R	S	R	S	R	S	R

Email

Name

Address

20__		20__		20__		20__		20__	
S	R	S	R	S	R	S	R	S	R

20__		20__		20__		20__		20__	
S	R	S	R	S	R	S	R	S	R

Email

Name

Address	20__		20__		20__		20__		20__	
	S	R	S	R	S	R	S	R	S	R
	20__		20__		20__		20__		20__	
	S	R	S	R	S	R	S	R	S	R
Email										

Name

Address	20__		20__		20__		20__		20__	
	S	R	S	R	S	R	S	R	S	R
	20__		20__		20__		20__		20__	
	S	R	S	R	S	R	S	R	S	R
Email										

Name

Address	20__		20__		20__		20__		20__	
	S	R	S	R	S	R	S	R	S	R
	20__		20__		20__		20__		20__	
	S	R	S	R	S	R	S	R	S	R
Email										

Name

Address	20__		20__		20__		20__		20__	
	S	R	S	R	S	R	S	R	S	R
	20__		20__		20__		20__		20__	
	S	R	S	R	S	R	S	R	S	R
Email										

Name

Address

20__		20__		20__		20__		20__	
S	R	S	R	S	R	S	R	S	R

20__		20__		20__		20__		20__	
S	R	S	R	S	R	S	R	S	R

Email

Name

Address

20__		20__		20__		20__		20__	
S	R	S	R	S	R	S	R	S	R

20__		20__		20__		20__		20__	
S	R	S	R	S	R	S	R	S	R

Email

Name

Address

20__		20__		20__		20__		20__	
S	R	S	R	S	R	S	R	S	R

20__		20__		20__		20__		20__	
S	R	S	R	S	R	S	R	S	R

Email

Name

Address

20__		20__		20__		20__		20__	
S	R	S	R	S	R	S	R	S	R

20__		20__		20__		20__		20__	
S	R	S	R	S	R	S	R	S	R

Email

A

Name										
Address	20__		20__		20__		20__		20__	
	S	R	S	R	S	R	S	R	S	R
	20__		20__		20__		20__		20__	
Email	S	R	S	R	S	R	S	R	S	R

Name										
Address	20__		20__		20__		20__		20__	
	S	R	S	R	S	R	S	R	S	R
	20__		20__		20__		20__		20__	
Email	S	R	S	R	S	R	S	R	S	R

Name										
Address	20__		20__		20__		20__		20__	
	S	R	S	R	S	R	S	R	S	R
	20__		20__		20__		20__		20__	
Email	S	R	S	R	S	R	S	R	S	R

Name										
Address	20__		20__		20__		20__		20__	
	S	R	S	R	S	R	S	R	S	R
	20__		20__		20__		20__		20__	
Email	S	R	S	R	S	R	S	R	S	R

B

Name										

Address	20__		20__		20__		20__		20__	
	S	R	S	R	S	R	S	R	S	R
	20__		20__		20__		20__		20__	
Email	S	R	S	R	S	R	S	R	S	R

Name										

Address	20__		20__		20__		20__		20__	
	S	R	S	R	S	R	S	R	S	R
	20__		20__		20__		20__		20__	
Email	S	R	S	R	S	R	S	R	S	R

Name										

Address	20__		20__		20__		20__		20__	
	S	R	S	R	S	R	S	R	S	R
	20__		20__		20__		20__		20__	
Email	S	R	S	R	S	R	S	R	S	R

Name										

Address	20__		20__		20__		20__		20__	
	S	R	S	R	S	R	S	R	S	R
	20__		20__		20__		20__		20__	
Email	S	R	S	R	S	R	S	R	S	R

Name

Address	20__		20__		20__		20__		20__	
	S	R	S	R	S	R	S	R	S	R
	20__		20__		20__		20__		20__	
Email	S	R	S	R	S	R	S	R	S	R

Name

Address	20__		20__		20__		20__		20__	
	S	R	S	R	S	R	S	R	S	R
	20__		20__		20__		20__		20__	
Email	S	R	S	R	S	R	S	R	S	R

Name

Address	20__		20__		20__		20__		20__	
	S	R	S	R	S	R	S	R	S	R
	20__		20__		20__		20__		20__	
Email	S	R	S	R	S	R	S	R	S	R

Name

Address	20__		20__		20__		20__		20__	
	S	R	S	R	S	R	S	R	S	R
	20__		20__		20__		20__		20__	
Email	S	R	S	R	S	R	S	R	S	R

Name

Address	20__		20__		20__		20__		20__	
	S	R	S	R	S	R	S	R	S	R
	20__		20__		20__		20__		20__	
Email	S	R	S	R	S	R	S	R	S	R

Name

Address	20__		20__		20__		20__		20__	
	S	R	S	R	S	R	S	R	S	R
	20__		20__		20__		20__		20__	
Email	S	R	S	R	S	R	S	R	S	R

Name

Address	20__		20__		20__		20__		20__	
	S	R	S	R	S	R	S	R	S	R
	20__		20__		20__		20__		20__	
Email	S	R	S	R	S	R	S	R	S	R

Name

Address	20__		20__		20__		20__		20__	
	S	R	S	R	S	R	S	R	S	R
	20__		20__		20__		20__		20__	
Email	S	R	S	R	S	R	S	R	S	R

B

Name

Address	20__		20__		20__		20__		20__	
	S	R	S	R	S	R	S	R	S	R
	20__		20__		20__		20__		20__	
Email	S	R	S	R	S	R	S	R	S	R

Name

Address	20__		20__		20__		20__		20__	
	S	R	S	R	S	R	S	R	S	R
	20__		20__		20__		20__		20__	
Email	S	R	S	R	S	R	S	R	S	R

Name

Address	20__		20__		20__		20__		20__	
	S	R	S	R	S	R	S	R	S	R
	20__		20__		20__		20__		20__	
Email	S	R	S	R	S	R	S	R	S	R

Name

Address	20__		20__		20__		20__		20__	
	S	R	S	R	S	R	S	R	S	R
	20__		20__		20__		20__		20__	
Email	S	R	S	R	S	R	S	R	S	R

B

Name

Address	20__		20__		20__		20__		20__	
	S	R	S	R	S	R	S	R	S	R
	20__		20__		20__		20__		20__	
Email	S	R	S	R	S	R	S	R	S	R

Name

Address	20__		20__		20__		20__		20__	
	S	R	S	R	S	R	S	R	S	R
	20__		20__		20__		20__		20__	
Email	S	R	S	R	S	R	S	R	S	R

Name

Address	20__		20__		20__		20__		20__	
	S	R	S	R	S	R	S	R	S	R
	20__		20__		20__		20__		20__	
Email	S	R	S	R	S	R	S	R	S	R

Name

Address	20__		20__		20__		20__		20__	
	S	R	S	R	S	R	S	R	S	R
	20__		20__		20__		20__		20__	
Email	S	R	S	R	S	R	S	R	S	R

Name

Address

20__		20__		20__		20__		20__	
S	R	S	R	S	R	S	R	S	R

20__		20__		20__		20__		20__	
S	R	S	R	S	R	S	R	S	R

Email

Name

Address

20__		20__		20__		20__		20__	
S	R	S	R	S	R	S	R	S	R

20__		20__		20__		20__		20__	
S	R	S	R	S	R	S	R	S	R

Email

Name

Address

20__		20__		20__		20__		20__	
S	R	S	R	S	R	S	R	S	R

20__		20__		20__		20__		20__	
S	R	S	R	S	R	S	R	S	R

Email

Name

Address

20__		20__		20__		20__		20__	
S	R	S	R	S	R	S	R	S	R

20__		20__		20__		20__		20__	
S	R	S	R	S	R	S	R	S	R

Email

Name	M Coleman										
Address		20__		20__		20__		20__		20__	
36 Queens Way		S	R	S	R	S	R	S	R	S	R
		✓									
		20__		20__		20__		20__		20__	
Email		S	R	S	R	S	R	S	R	S	R

Name											
Address		20__		20__		20__		20__		20__	
		S	R	S	R	S	R	S	R	S	R
		20__		20__		20__		20__		20__	
Email		S	R	S	R	S	R	S	R	S	R

Name											
Address		20__		20__		20__		20__		20__	
		S	R	S	R	S	R	S	R	S	R
		20__		20__		20__		20__		20__	
Email		S	R	S	R	S	R	S	R	S	R

Name											
Address		20__		20__		20__		20__		20__	
		S	R	S	R	S	R	S	R	S	R
		20__		20__		20__		20__		20__	
Email		S	R	S	R	S	R	S	R	S	R

C

Name										

Address	20__		20__		20__		20__		20__	
	S	R	S	R	S	R	S	R	S	R
	20__		20__		20__		20__		20__	
Email	S	R	S	R	S	R	S	R	S	R

Name										

Address	20__		20__		20__		20__		20__	
	S	R	S	R	S	R	S	R	S	R
	20__		20__		20__		20__		20__	
Email	S	R	S	R	S	R	S	R	S	R

Name										

Address	20__		20__		20__		20__		20__	
	S	R	S	R	S	R	S	R	S	R
	20__		20__		20__		20__		20__	
Email	S	R	S	R	S	R	S	R	S	R

Name										

Address	20__		20__		20__		20__		20__	
	S	R	S	R	S	R	S	R	S	R
	20__		20__		20__		20__		20__	
Email	S	R	S	R	S	R	S	R	S	R

C

Name

Address	20__		20__		20__		20__		20__	
	S	R	S	R	S	R	S	R	S	R
	20__		20__		20__		20__		20__	
Email	S	R	S	R	S	R	S	R	S	R

Name

Address	20__		20__		20__		20__		20__	
	S	R	S	R	S	R	S	R	S	R
	20__		20__		20__		20__		20__	
Email	S	R	S	R	S	R	S	R	S	R

Name

Address	20__		20__		20__		20__		20__	
	S	R	S	R	S	R	S	R	S	R
	20__		20__		20__		20__		20__	
Email	S	R	S	R	S	R	S	R	S	R

Name

Address	20__		20__		20__		20__		20__	
	S	R	S	R	S	R	S	R	S	R
	20__		20__		20__		20__		20__	
Email	S	R	S	R	S	R	S	R	S	R

Name										

Address	20__		20__		20__		20__		20__	
	S	R	S	R	S	R	S	R	S	R
	20__		20__		20__		20__		20__	
Email	S	R	S	R	S	R	S	R	S	R

Name										

Address	20__		20__		20__		20__		20__	
	S	R	S	R	S	R	S	R	S	R
	20__		20__		20__		20__		20__	
Email	S	R	S	R	S	R	S	R	S	R

Name										

Address	20__		20__		20__		20__		20__	
	S	R	S	R	S	R	S	R	S	R
	20__		20__		20__		20__		20__	
Email	S	R	S	R	S	R	S	R	S	R

Name										

Address	20__		20__		20__		20__		20__	
	S	R	S	R	S	R	S	R	S	R
	20__		20__		20__		20__		20__	
Email	S	R	S	R	S	R	S	R	S	R

Name										

Address	20__		20__		20__		20__		20__	
	S	R	S	R	S	R	S	R	S	R
	20__		20__		20__		20__		20__	
Email	S	R	S	R	S	R	S	R	S	R

Name										

Address	20__		20__		20__		20__		20__	
	S	R	S	R	S	R	S	R	S	R
	20__		20__		20__		20__		20__	
Email	S	R	S	R	S	R	S	R	S	R

Name										

Address	20__		20__		20__		20__		20__	
	S	R	S	R	S	R	S	R	S	R
	20__		20__		20__		20__		20__	
Email	S	R	S	R	S	R	S	R	S	R

Name										

Address	20__		20__		20__		20__		20__	
	S	R	S	R	S	R	S	R	S	R
	20__		20__		20__		20__		20__	
Email	S	R	S	R	S	R	S	R	S	R

Name										
Address	20__		20__		20__		20__		20__	
	S	R	S	R	S	R	S	R	S	R
	20__		20__		20__		20__		20__	
Email	S	R	S	R	S	R	S	R	S	R

Name										
Address	20__		20__		20__		20__		20__	
	S	R	S	R	S	R	S	R	S	R
	20__		20__		20__		20__		20__	
Email	S	R	S	R	S	R	S	R	S	R

Name										
Address	20__		20__		20__		20__		20__	
	S	R	S	R	S	R	S	R	S	R
	20__		20__		20__		20__		20__	
Email	S	R	S	R	S	R	S	R	S	R

Name										
Address	20__		20__		20__		20__		20__	
	S	R	S	R	S	R	S	R	S	R
	20__		20__		20__		20__		20__	
Email	S	R	S	R	S	R	S	R	S	R

Name	Jean Davis										
Address 12 Alcock Crest Warminster		20__		20__		20__		20__		20__	
		S	R	S	R	S	R	S	R	S	R
		20__		20__		20__		20__		20__	
Email		S	R	S	R	S	R	S	R	S	R

Name											
Address Ann & John Shirley Steve		20 22	20__		20__		20__		20__		
		8	R	S	R	S	R	S	R	S	R
		20__		20__		20__		20__		20__	
Email		S	R	S	R	S	R	S	R	S	R

Name											
Address		20__		20__		20__		20__		20__	
		S	R	S	R	S	R	S	R	S	R
		20__		20__		20__		20__		20__	
Email		S	R	S	R	S	R	S	R	S	R

Name											
Address		20__		20__		20__		20__		20__	
		S	R	S	R	S	R	S	R	S	R
		20__		20__		20__		20__		20__	
Email		S	R	S	R	S	R	S	R	S	R

D

Name										

Address	20__		20__		20__		20__		20__	
	S	R	S	R	S	R	S	R	S	R
	20__		20__		20__		20__		20__	
Email	S	R	S	R	S	R	S	R	S	R

Name										

Address	20__		20__		20__		20__		20__	
	S	R	S	R	S	R	S	R	S	R
	20__		20__		20__		20__		20__	
Email	S	R	S	R	S	R	S	R	S	R

Name										

Address	20__		20__		20__		20__		20__	
	S	R	S	R	S	R	S	R	S	R
	20__		20__		20__		20__		20__	
Email	S	R	S	R	S	R	S	R	S	R

Name										

Address	20__		20__		20__		20__		20__	
	S	R	S	R	S	R	S	R	S	R
	20__		20__		20__		20__		20__	
Email	S	R	S	R	S	R	S	R	S	R

Name

Address	20__		20__		20__		20__		20__	
	S	R	S	R	S	R	S	R	S	R
	20__		20__		20__		20__		20__	
Email	S	R	S	R	S	R	S	R	S	R

Name

Address	20__		20__		20__		20__		20__	
	S	R	S	R	S	R	S	R	S	R
	20__		20__		20__		20__		20__	
Email	S	R	S	R	S	R	S	R	S	R

Name

Address	20__		20__		20__		20__		20__	
	S	R	S	R	S	R	S	R	S	R
	20__		20__		20__		20__		20__	
Email	S	R	S	R	S	R	S	R	S	R

Name

Address	20__		20__		20__		20__		20__	
	S	R	S	R	S	R	S	R	S	R
	20__		20__		20__		20__		20__	
Email	S	R	S	R	S	R	S	R	S	R

D

Name

Address	20__		20__		20__		20__		20__	
	S	R	S	R	S	R	S	R	S	R
	20__		20__		20__		20__		20__	
Email	S	R	S	R	S	R	S	R	S	R

Name

Address	20__		20__		20__		20__		20__	
	S	R	S	R	S	R	S	R	S	R
	20__		20__		20__		20__		20__	
Email	S	R	S	R	S	R	S	R	S	R

Name

Address	20__		20__		20__		20__		20__	
	S	R	S	R	S	R	S	R	S	R
	20__		20__		20__		20__		20__	
Email	S	R	S	R	S	R	S	R	S	R

Name

Address	20__		20__		20__		20__		20__	
	S	R	S	R	S	R	S	R	S	R
	20__		20__		20__		20__		20__	
Email	S	R	S	R	S	R	S	R	S	R

D

Name											

Address	20__		20__		20__		20__		20__	
	S	R	S	R	S	R	S	R	S	R
	20__		20__		20__		20__		20__	
Email	S	R	S	R	S	R	S	R	S	R

Name											

Address	20__		20__		20__		20__		20__	
	S	R	S	R	S	R	S	R	S	R
	20__		20__		20__		20__		20__	
Email	S	R	S	R	S	R	S	R	S	R

Name											

Address	20__		20__		20__		20__		20__	
	S	R	S	R	S	R	S	R	S	R
	20__		20__		20__		20__		20__	
Email	S	R	S	R	S	R	S	R	S	R

Name											

Address	20__		20__		20__		20__		20__	
	S	R	S	R	S	R	S	R	S	R
	20__		20__		20__		20__		20__	
Email	S	R	S	R	S	R	S	R	S	R

D

Name										

Address	20__		20__		20__		20__		20__	
	S	R	S	R	S	R	S	R	S	R
	20__		20__		20__		20__		20__	
Email	S	R	S	R	S	R	S	R	S	R

Name										

Address	20__		20__		20__		20__		20__	
	S	R	S	R	S	R	S	R	S	R
	20__		20__		20__		20__		20__	
Email	S	R	S	R	S	R	S	R	S	R

Name										

Address	20__		20__		20__		20__		20__	
	S	R	S	R	S	R	S	R	S	R
	20__		20__		20__		20__		20__	
Email	S	R	S	R	S	R	S	R	S	R

Name										

Address	20__		20__		20__		20__		20__	
	S	R	S	R	S	R	S	R	S	R
	20__		20__		20__		20__		20__	
Email	S	R	S	R	S	R	S	R	S	R

Name										
Address	20__		20__		20__		20__		20__	
	S	R	S	R	S	R	S	R	S	R
	20__		20__		20__		20__		20__	
Email	S	R	S	R	S	R	S	R	S	R

Name										
Address	20__		20__		20__		20__		20__	
	S	R	S	R	S	R	S	R	S	R
	20__		20__		20__		20__		20__	
Email	S	R	S	R	S	R	S	R	S	R

Name										
Address	20__		20__		20__		20__		20__	
	S	R	S	R	S	R	S	R	S	R
	20__		20__		20__		20__		20__	
Email	S	R	S	R	S	R	S	R	S	R

Name										
Address	20__		20__		20__		20__		20__	
	S	R	S	R	S	R	S	R	S	R
	20__		20__		20__		20__		20__	
Email	S	R	S	R	S	R	S	R	S	R

E

Name											

Address	20__		20__		20__		20__		20__	
	S	R	S	R	S	R	S	R	S	R
	20__		20__		20__		20__		20__	
Email	S	R	S	R	S	R	S	R	S	R

Name											

Address	20__		20__		20__		20__		20__	
	S	R	S	R	S	R	S	R	S	R
	20__		20__		20__		20__		20__	
Email	S	R	S	R	S	R	S	R	S	R

Name											

Address	20__		20__		20__		20__		20__	
	S	R	S	R	S	R	S	R	S	R
	20__		20__		20__		20__		20__	
Email	S	R	S	R	S	R	S	R	S	R

Name											

Address	20__		20__		20__		20__		20__	
	S	R	S	R	S	R	S	R	S	R
	20__		20__		20__		20__		20__	
Email	S	R	S	R	S	R	S	R	S	R

E

Name											

Entry 1

Address	20__		20__		20__		20__		20__	
	S	R	S	R	S	R	S	R	S	R
	20__		20__		20__		20__		20__	
Email	S	R	S	R	S	R	S	R	S	R

Entry 2

Name											

Address	20__		20__		20__		20__		20__	
	S	R	S	R	S	R	S	R	S	R
	20__		20__		20__		20__		20__	
Email	S	R	S	R	S	R	S	R	S	R

Entry 3

Name											

Address	20__		20__		20__		20__		20__	
	S	R	S	R	S	R	S	R	S	R
	20__		20__		20__		20__		20__	
Email	S	R	S	R	S	R	S	R	S	R

Entry 4

Name											

Address	20__		20__		20__		20__		20__	
	S	R	S	R	S	R	S	R	S	R
	20__		20__		20__		20__		20__	
Email	S	R	S	R	S	R	S	R	S	R

E

Name

Address	20__		20__		20__		20__		20__	
	S	R	S	R	S	R	S	R	S	R
	20__		20__		20__		20__		20__	
Email	S	R	S	R	S	R	S	R	S	R

Name

Address	20__		20__		20__		20__		20__	
	S	R	S	R	S	R	S	R	S	R
	20__		20__		20__		20__		20__	
Email	S	R	S	R	S	R	S	R	S	R

Name

Address	20__		20__		20__		20__		20__	
	S	R	S	R	S	R	S	R	S	R
	20__		20__		20__		20__		20__	
Email	S	R	S	R	S	R	S	R	S	R

Name

Address	20__		20__		20__		20__		20__	
	S	R	S	R	S	R	S	R	S	R
	20__		20__		20__		20__		20__	
Email	S	R	S	R	S	R	S	R	S	R

Name

Address	20__		20__		20__		20__		20__	
	S	R	S	R	S	R	S	R	S	R
	20__		20__		20__		20__		20__	
Email	S	R	S	R	S	R	S	R	S	R

Name

Address	20__		20__		20__		20__		20__	
	S	R	S	R	S	R	S	R	S	R
	20__		20__		20__		20__		20__	
Email	S	R	S	R	S	R	S	R	S	R

Name

Address	20__		20__		20__		20__		20__	
	S	R	S	R	S	R	S	R	S	R
	20__		20__		20__		20__		20__	
Email	S	R	S	R	S	R	S	R	S	R

Name

Address	20__		20__		20__		20__		20__	
	S	R	S	R	S	R	S	R	S	R
	20__		20__		20__		20__		20__	
Email	S	R	S	R	S	R	S	R	S	R

E

Name

Address	20__		20__		20__		20__		20__	
	S	R	S	R	S	R	S	R	S	R
	20__		20__		20__		20__		20__	
Email	S	R	S	R	S	R	S	R	S	R

Name

Address	20__		20__		20__		20__		20__	
	S	R	S	R	S	R	S	R	S	R
	20__		20__		20__		20__		20__	
Email	S	R	S	R	S	R	S	R	S	R

Name

Address	20__		20__		20__		20__		20__	
	S	R	S	R	S	R	S	R	S	R
	20__		20__		20__		20__		20__	
Email	S	R	S	R	S	R	S	R	S	R

Name

Address	20__		20__		20__		20__		20__	
	S	R	S	R	S	R	S	R	S	R
	20__		20__		20__		20__		20__	
Email	S	R	S	R	S	R	S	R	S	R

F

Name										

Name

Address	20__		20__		20__		20__		20__	
	S	R	S	R	S	R	S	R	S	R
	20__		20__		20__		20__		20__	
Email	S	R	S	R	S	R	S	R	S	R

Name

Address	20__		20__		20__		20__		20__	
	S	R	S	R	S	R	S	R	S	R
	20__		20__		20__		20__		20__	
Email	S	R	S	R	S	R	S	R	S	R

Name

Address	20__		20__		20__		20__		20__	
	S	R	S	R	S	R	S	R	S	R
	20__		20__		20__		20__		20__	
Email	S	R	S	R	S	R	S	R	S	R

Name

Address	20__		20__		20__		20__		20__	
	S	R	S	R	S	R	S	R	S	R
	20__		20__		20__		20__		20__	
Email	S	R	S	R	S	R	S	R	S	R

F

Name										

Address	20__		20__		20__		20__		20__	
	S	R	S	R	S	R	S	R	S	R
	20__		20__		20__		20__		20__	
Email	S	R	S	R	S	R	S	R	S	R

Name										

Address	20__		20__		20__		20__		20__	
	S	R	S	R	S	R	S	R	S	R
	20__		20__		20__		20__		20__	
Email	S	R	S	R	S	R	S	R	S	R

Name										

Address	20__		20__		20__		20__		20__	
	S	R	S	R	S	R	S	R	S	R
	20__		20__		20__		20__		20__	
Email	S	R	S	R	S	R	S	R	S	R

Name										

Address	20__		20__		20__		20__		20__	
	S	R	S	R	S	R	S	R	S	R
	20__		20__		20__		20__		20__	
Email	S	R	S	R	S	R	S	R	S	R

F

Name										
Address	20__		20__		20__		20__		20__	
	S	R	S	R	S	R	S	R	S	R
	20__		20__		20__		20__		20__	
Email	S	R	S	R	S	R	S	R	S	R

Name										
Address	20__		20__		20__		20__		20__	
	S	R	S	R	S	R	S	R	S	R
	20__		20__		20__		20__		20__	
Email	S	R	S	R	S	R	S	R	S	R

Name										
Address	20__		20__		20__		20__		20__	
	S	R	S	R	S	R	S	R	S	R
	20__		20__		20__		20__		20__	
Email	S	R	S	R	S	R	S	R	S	R

Name										
Address	20__		20__		20__		20__		20__	
	S	R	S	R	S	R	S	R	S	R
	20__		20__		20__		20__		20__	
Email	S	R	S	R	S	R	S	R	S	R

	F

Name Derek

Address	20 2?		20__		20__		20__		20__	
7 Robin Close	S	R	S	R	S	R	S	R	S	R
Warminster	✓									
	20__		20__		20__		20__		20__	
Email	S	R	S	R	S	R	S	R	S	R

Name Julie

Address 19 Wedmerd Clo	2021		20__		20__		20__		20__	
Frome	S	R	S	R	S	R	S	R	S	R
19 Wedmore Close										
	20__		20__		20__		20__		20__	
Email	S	R	S	R	S	R	S	R	S	R

Name Alison

Address 65 St Johns Rd	2021		20__		20__		20__		20__	
Warminster	S	R	S	R	S	R	S	R	S	R
	20__		20__		20__		20__		20__	
Email	S	R	S	R	S	R	S	R	S	R

Name Lauren

Address 24	20__		20__		20__		20__		20__	
Frome	S	R	S	R	S	R	S	R	S	R
Rowan Court										
	20__		20__		20__		20__		20__	
Email	S	R	S	R	S	R	S	R	S	R

Name Katy

Address	20__		20__		20__		20__		20__	
	S	R	S	R	S	R	S	R	S	R
	20__		20__		20__		20__		20__	
Email	S	R	S	R	S	R	S	R	S	R

Name Hannah

Address	20__		20__		20__		20__		20__	
	S	R	S	R	S	R	S	R	S	R
	20__		20__		20__		20__		20__	
Email	S	R	S	R	S	R	S	R	S	R

Name

Address Carol Fletcher	20__		20__		20__		20__		20__	
Gwen	S	R	S	R	S	R	S	R	S	R
Maureen	20__		20__		20__		20__		20__	
Email	S	R	S	R	S	R	S	R	S	R

Name

Address	20__		20__		20__		20__		20__	
	S	R	S	R	S	R	S	R	S	R
	20__		20__		20__		20__		20__	
Email	S	R	S	R	S	R	S	R	S	R

F

Name

Address	20__		20__		20__		20__		20__	
	S	R	S	R	S	R	S	R	S	R
	20__		20__		20__		20__		20__	
Email	S	R	S	R	S	R	S	R	S	R

Name

Address	20__		20__		20__		20__		20__	
	S	R	S	R	S	R	S	R	S	R
	20__		20__		20__		20__		20__	
Email	S	R	S	R	S	R	S	R	S	R

Name

Address	20__		20__		20__		20__		20__	
	S	R	S	R	S	R	S	R	S	R
	20__		20__		20__		20__		20__	
Email	S	R	S	R	S	R	S	R	S	R

Name

Address	20__		20__		20__		20__		20__	
	S	R	S	R	S	R	S	R	S	R
	20__		20__		20__		20__		20__	
Email	S	R	S	R	S	R	S	R	S	R

Name										
Address	20__		20__		20__		20__		20__	
	S	R	S	R	S	R	S	R	S	R
	20__		20__		20__		20__		20__	
Email	S	R	S	R	S	R	S	R	S	R

Name										
Address	20__		20__		20__		20__		20__	
	S	R	S	R	S	R	S	R	S	R
	20__		20__		20__		20__		20__	
Email	S	R	S	R	S	R	S	R	S	R

Name										
Address	20__		20__		20__		20__		20__	
	S	R	S	R	S	R	S	R	S	R
	20__		20__		20__		20__		20__	
Email	S	R	S	R	S	R	S	R	S	R

Name										
Address	20__		20__		20__		20__		20__	
	S	R	S	R	S	R	S	R	S	R
	20__		20__		20__		20__		20__	
Email	S	R	S	R	S	R	S	R	S	R

G

Name											
Address		20__		20__		20__		20__		20__	
		S	R	S	R	S	R	S	R	S	R
		20__		20__		20__		20__		20__	
Email		S	R	S	R	S	R	S	R	S	R

Name											
Address		20__		20__		20__		20__		20__	
		S	R	S	R	S	R	S	R	S	R
		20__		20__		20__		20__		20__	
Email		S	R	S	R	S	R	S	R	S	R

Name											
Address		20__		20__		20__		20__		20__	
		S	R	S	R	S	R	S	R	S	R
		20__		20__		20__		20__		20__	
Email		S	R	S	R	S	R	S	R	S	R

Name											
Address		20__		20__		20__		20__		20__	
		S	R	S	R	S	R	S	R	S	R
		20__		20__		20__		20__		20__	
Email		S	R	S	R	S	R	S	R	S	R

Name

Address	20__		20__		20__		20__		20__	
	S	R	S	R	S	R	S	R	S	R
	20__		20__		20__		20__		20__	
Email	S	R	S	R	S	R	S	R	S	R

Name

Address	20__		20__		20__		20__		20__	
	S	R	S	R	S	R	S	R	S	R
	20__		20__		20__		20__		20__	
Email	S	R	S	R	S	R	S	R	S	R

Name

Address	20__		20__		20__		20__		20__	
	S	R	S	R	S	R	S	R	S	R
	20__		20__		20__		20__		20__	
Email	S	R	S	R	S	R	S	R	S	R

Name

Address	20__		20__		20__		20__		20__	
	S	R	S	R	S	R	S	R	S	R
	20__		20__		20__		20__		20__	
Email	S	R	S	R	S	R	S	R	S	R

G

Name											

Address	20__		20__		20__		20__		20__	
	S	R	S	R	S	R	S	R	S	R
	20__		20__		20__		20__		20__	
Email	S	R	S	R	S	R	S	R	S	R

Name											

Address	20__		20__		20__		20__		20__	
	S	R	S	R	S	R	S	R	S	R
	20__		20__		20__		20__		20__	
Email	S	R	S	R	S	R	S	R	S	R

Name											

Address	20__		20__		20__		20__		20__	
	S	R	S	R	S	R	S	R	S	R
	20__		20__		20__		20__		20__	
Email	S	R	S	R	S	R	S	R	S	R

Name											

Address	20__		20__		20__		20__		20__	
	S	R	S	R	S	R	S	R	S	R
	20__		20__		20__		20__		20__	
Email	S	R	S	R	S	R	S	R	S	R

Name										
Address	20__		20__		20__		20__		20__	
	S	R	S	R	S	R	S	R	S	R
	20__		20__		20__		20__		20__	
Email	S	R	S	R	S	R	S	R	S	R

Name										
Address	20__		20__		20__		20__		20__	
	S	R	S	R	S	R	S	R	S	R
	20__		20__		20__		20__		20__	
Email	S	R	S	R	S	R	S	R	S	R

Name										
Address	20__		20__		20__		20__		20__	
	S	R	S	R	S	R	S	R	S	R
	20__		20__		20__		20__		20__	
Email	S	R	S	R	S	R	S	R	S	R

Name										
Address	20__		20__		20__		20__		20__	
	S	R	S	R	S	R	S	R	S	R
	20__		20__		20__		20__		20__	
Email	S	R	S	R	S	R	S	R	S	R

G

Name										

Address	20__		20__		20__		20__		20__	
	S	R	S	R	S	R	S	R	S	R
	20__		20__		20__		20__		20__	
Email	S	R	S	R	S	R	S	R	S	R

Name										

Address	20__		20__		20__		20__		20__	
	S	R	S	R	S	R	S	R	S	R
	20__		20__		20__		20__		20__	
Email	S	R	S	R	S	R	S	R	S	R

Name										

Address	20__		20__		20__		20__		20__	
	S	R	S	R	S	R	S	R	S	R
	20__		20__		20__		20__		20__	
Email	S	R	S	R	S	R	S	R	S	R

Name										

Address	20__		20__		20__		20__		20__	
	S	R	S	R	S	R	S	R	S	R
	20__		20__		20__		20__		20__	
Email	S	R	S	R	S	R	S	R	S	R

Name										
S Hulse										

Address	20__		20__		20__		20__		20__	
15. Hemlbregt Vale	S	R	S	R	S	R	S	R	S	R
Helysby										
Frodsham Cheshire	20__		20__		20__		20__		20__	
Email WA6 ODB	S	R	S	R	S	R	S	R	S	R

Name										

Address	20__		20__		20__		20__		20__	
	S	R	S	R	S	R	S	R	S	R
	20__		20__		20__		20__		20__	
Email	S	R	S	R	S	R	S	R	S	R

Name										

Address	20__		20__		20__		20__		20__	
	S	R	S	R	S	R	S	R	S	R
	20__		20__		20__		20__		20__	
Email	S	R	S	R	S	R	S	R	S	R

Name										

Address	20__		20__		20__		20__		20__	
	S	R	S	R	S	R	S	R	S	R
	20__		20__		20__		20__		20__	
Email	S	R	S	R	S	R	S	R	S	R

H

Name

Address	20__		20__		20__		20__		20__	
	S	R	S	R	S	R	S	R	S	R
	20__		20__		20__		20__		20__	
Email	S	R	S	R	S	R	S	R	S	R

Name

Address	20__		20__		20__		20__		20__	
	S	R	S	R	S	R	S	R	S	R
	20__		20__		20__		20__		20__	
Email	S	R	S	R	S	R	S	R	S	R

Name

Address	20__		20__		20__		20__		20__	
	S	R	S	R	S	R	S	R	S	R
	20__		20__		20__		20__		20__	
Email	S	R	S	R	S	R	S	R	S	R

Name

Address	20__		20__		20__		20__		20__	
	S	R	S	R	S	R	S	R	S	R
	20__		20__		20__		20__		20__	
Email	S	R	S	R	S	R	S	R	S	R

H

Name

Address	20__		20__		20__		20__		20__	
	S	R	S	R	S	R	S	R	S	R
	20__		20__		20__		20__		20__	
Email	S	R	S	R	S	R	S	R	S	R

Name

Address	20__		20__		20__		20__		20__	
	S	R	S	R	S	R	S	R	S	R
	20__		20__		20__		20__		20__	
Email	S	R	S	R	S	R	S	R	S	R

Name

Address	20__		20__		20__		20__		20__	
	S	R	S	R	S	R	S	R	S	R
	20__		20__		20__		20__		20__	
Email	S	R	S	R	S	R	S	R	S	R

Name

Address	20__		20__		20__		20__		20__	
	S	R	S	R	S	R	S	R	S	R
	20__		20__		20__		20__		20__	
Email	S	R	S	R	S	R	S	R	S	R

H

Name										

Address	20__		20__		20__		20__		20__	
	S	R	S	R	S	R	S	R	S	R
	20__		20__		20__		20__		20__	
Email	S	R	S	R	S	R	S	R	S	R

Name										

Address	20__		20__		20__		20__		20__	
	S	R	S	R	S	R	S	R	S	R
	20__		20__		20__		20__		20__	
Email	S	R	S	R	S	R	S	R	S	R

Name										

Address	20__		20__		20__		20__		20__	
	S	R	S	R	S	R	S	R	S	R
	20__		20__		20__		20__		20__	
Email	S	R	S	R	S	R	S	R	S	R

Name										

Address	20__		20__		20__		20__		20__	
	S	R	S	R	S	R	S	R	S	R
	20__		20__		20__		20__		20__	
Email	S	R	S	R	S	R	S	R	S	R

H

Name										
Address	20__		20__		20__		20__		20__	
	S	R	S	R	S	R	S	R	S	R
	20__		20__		20__		20__		20__	
Email	S	R	S	R	S	R	S	R	S	R

Name										
Address	20__		20__		20__		20__		20__	
	S	R	S	R	S	R	S	R	S	R
	20__		20__		20__		20__		20__	
Email	S	R	S	R	S	R	S	R	S	R

Name										
Address	20__		20__		20__		20__		20__	
	S	R	S	R	S	R	S	R	S	R
	20__		20__		20__		20__		20__	
Email	S	R	S	R	S	R	S	R	S	R

Name										
Address	20__		20__		20__		20__		20__	
	S	R	S	R	S	R	S	R	S	R
	20__		20__		20__		20__		20__	
Email	S	R	S	R	S	R	S	R	S	R

Name										
Address	20__		20__		20__		20__		20__	
	S	R	S	R	S	R	S	R	S	R
	20__		20__		20__		20__		20__	
Email	S	R	S	R	S	R	S	R	S	R

Name										
Address	20__		20__		20__		20__		20__	
	S	R	S	R	S	R	S	R	S	R
	20__		20__		20__		20__		20__	
Email	S	R	S	R	S	R	S	R	S	R

Name										
Address	20__		20__		20__		20__		20__	
	S	R	S	R	S	R	S	R	S	R
	20__		20__		20__		20__		20__	
Email	S	R	S	R	S	R	S	R	S	R

Name										
Address	20__		20__		20__		20__		20__	
	S	R	S	R	S	R	S	R	S	R
	20__		20__		20__		20__		20__	
Email	S	R	S	R	S	R	S	R	S	R

Name

Address	20__		20__		20__		20__		20__	
	S	R	S	R	S	R	S	R	S	R
	20__		20__		20__		20__		20__	
Email	S	R	S	R	S	R	S	R	S	R

Name

Address	20__		20__		20__		20__		20__	
	S	R	S	R	S	R	S	R	S	R
	20__		20__		20__		20__		20__	
Email	S	R	S	R	S	R	S	R	S	R

Name

Address	20__		20__		20__		20__		20__	
	S	R	S	R	S	R	S	R	S	R
	20__		20__		20__		20__		20__	
Email	S	R	S	R	S	R	S	R	S	R

Name

Address	20__		20__		20__		20__		20__	
	S	R	S	R	S	R	S	R	S	R
	20__		20__		20__		20__		20__	
Email	S	R	S	R	S	R	S	R	S	R

1

Name

Address	20__		20__		20__		20__		20__	
	S	R	S	R	S	R	S	R	S	R
	20__		20__		20__		20__		20__	
	S	R	S	R	S	R	S	R	S	R
Email										

Name

Address	20__		20__		20__		20__		20__	
	S	R	S	R	S	R	S	R	S	R
	20__		20__		20__		20__		20__	
	S	R	S	R	S	R	S	R	S	R
Email										

Name

Address	20__		20__		20__		20__		20__	
	S	R	S	R	S	R	S	R	S	R
	20__		20__		20__		20__		20__	
	S	R	S	R	S	R	S	R	S	R
Email										

Name

Address	20__		20__		20__		20__		20__	
	S	R	S	R	S	R	S	R	S	R
	20__		20__		20__		20__		20__	
	S	R	S	R	S	R	S	R	S	R
Email										

Name

Address	20__		20__		20__		20__		20__	
	S	R	S	R	S	R	S	R	S	R
	20__		20__		20__		20__		20__	
Email	S	R	S	R	S	R	S	R	S	R

Name

Address	20__		20__		20__		20__		20__	
	S	R	S	R	S	R	S	R	S	R
	20__		20__		20__		20__		20__	
Email	S	R	S	R	S	R	S	R	S	R

Name

Address	20__		20__		20__		20__		20__	
	S	R	S	R	S	R	S	R	S	R
	20__		20__		20__		20__		20__	
Email	S	R	S	R	S	R	S	R	S	R

Name

Address	20__		20__		20__		20__		20__	
	S	R	S	R	S	R	S	R	S	R
	20__		20__		20__		20__		20__	
Email	S	R	S	R	S	R	S	R	S	R

Name

Address	20__		20__		20__		20__		20__	
	S	R	S	R	S	R	S	R	S	R
	20__		20__		20__		20__		20__	
Email	S	R	S	R	S	R	S	R	S	R

Name

Address	20__		20__		20__		20__		20__	
	S	R	S	R	S	R	S	R	S	R
	20__		20__		20__		20__		20__	
Email	S	R	S	R	S	R	S	R	S	R

Name

Address	20__		20__		20__		20__		20__	
	S	R	S	R	S	R	S	R	S	R
	20__		20__		20__		20__		20__	
Email	S	R	S	R	S	R	S	R	S	R

Name

Address	20__		20__		20__		20__		20__	
	S	R	S	R	S	R	S	R	S	R
	20__		20__		20__		20__		20__	
Email	S	R	S	R	S	R	S	R	S	R

Name

Address	20__		20__		20__		20__		20__	
	S	R	S	R	S	R	S	R	S	R
	20__		20__		20__		20__		20__	
Email	S	R	S	R	S	R	S	R	S	R

Name

Address	20__		20__		20__		20__		20__	
	S	R	S	R	S	R	S	R	S	R
	20__		20__		20__		20__		20__	
Email	S	R	S	R	S	R	S	R	S	R

Name

Address	20__		20__		20__		20__		20__	
	S	R	S	R	S	R	S	R	S	R
	20__		20__		20__		20__		20__	
Email	S	R	S	R	S	R	S	R	S	R

Name

Address	20__		20__		20__		20__		20__	
	S	R	S	R	S	R	S	R	S	R
	20__		20__		20__		20__		20__	
Email	S	R	S	R	S	R	S	R	S	R

I	

Entry 1

Name										
Address	20__		20__		20__		20__		20__	
	S	R	S	R	S	R	S	R	S	R
	20__		20__		20__		20__		20__	
Email	S	R	S	R	S	R	S	R	S	R

Entry 2

Name										
Address	20__		20__		20__		20__		20__	
	S	R	S	R	S	R	S	R	S	R
	20__		20__		20__		20__		20__	
Email	S	R	S	R	S	R	S	R	S	R

Entry 3

Name										
Address	20__		20__		20__		20__		20__	
	S	R	S	R	S	R	S	R	S	R
	20__		20__		20__		20__		20__	
Email	S	R	S	R	S	R	S	R	S	R

Entry 4

Name										
Address	20__		20__		20__		20__		20__	
	S	R	S	R	S	R	S	R	S	R
	20__		20__		20__		20__		20__	
Email	S	R	S	R	S	R	S	R	S	R

J

Name

Address

20__		20__		20__		20__		20__	
S	R	S	R	S	R	S	R	S	R

20__		20__		20__		20__		20__	
S	R	S	R	S	R	S	R	S	R

Email

Name

Address

20__		20__		20__		20__		20__	
S	R	S	R	S	R	S	R	S	R

20__		20__		20__		20__		20__	
S	R	S	R	S	R	S	R	S	R

Email

Name

Address

20__		20__		20__		20__		20__	
S	R	S	R	S	R	S	R	S	R

20__		20__		20__		20__		20__	
S	R	S	R	S	R	S	R	S	R

Email

Name

Address

20__		20__		20__		20__		20__	
S	R	S	R	S	R	S	R	S	R

20__		20__		20__		20__		20__	
S	R	S	R	S	R	S	R	S	R

Email

J

Name										
Address	20__		20__		20__		20__		20__	
	S	R	S	R	S	R	S	R	S	R
	20__		20__		20__		20__		20__	
Email	S	R	S	R	S	R	S	R	S	R

Name										
Address	20__		20__		20__		20__		20__	
	S	R	S	R	S	R	S	R	S	R
	20__		20__		20__		20__		20__	
Email	S	R	S	R	S	R	S	R	S	R

Name										
Address	20__		20__		20__		20__		20__	
	S	R	S	R	S	R	S	R	S	R
	20__		20__		20__		20__		20__	
Email	S	R	S	R	S	R	S	R	S	R

Name										
Address	20__		20__		20__		20__		20__	
	S	R	S	R	S	R	S	R	S	R
	20__		20__		20__		20__		20__	
Email	S	R	S	R	S	R	S	R	S	R

J

Name										
Address	20__		20__		20__		20__		20__	
	S	R	S	R	S	R	S	R	S	R
	20__		20__		20__		20__		20__	
Email	S	R	S	R	S	R	S	R	S	R

Name										
Address	20__		20__		20__		20__		20__	
	S	R	S	R	S	R	S	R	S	R
	20__		20__		20__		20__		20__	
Email	S	R	S	R	S	R	S	R	S	R

Name										
Address	20__		20__		20__		20__		20__	
	S	R	S	R	S	R	S	R	S	R
	20__		20__		20__		20__		20__	
Email	S	R	S	R	S	R	S	R	S	R

Name										
Address	20__		20__		20__		20__		20__	
	S	R	S	R	S	R	S	R	S	R
	20__		20__		20__		20__		20__	
Email	S	R	S	R	S	R	S	R	S	R

J

Name

Address	20__		20__		20__		20__		20__	
	S	R	S	R	S	R	S	R	S	R
	20__		20__		20__		20__		20__	
Email	S	R	S	R	S	R	S	R	S	R

Name

Address	20__		20__		20__		20__		20__	
	S	R	S	R	S	R	S	R	S	R
	20__		20__		20__		20__		20__	
Email	S	R	S	R	S	R	S	R	S	R

Name

Address	20__		20__		20__		20__		20__	
	S	R	S	R	S	R	S	R	S	R
	20__		20__		20__		20__		20__	
Email	S	R	S	R	S	R	S	R	S	R

Name

Address	20__		20__		20__		20__		20__	
	S	R	S	R	S	R	S	R	S	R
	20__		20__		20__		20__		20__	
Email	S	R	S	R	S	R	S	R	S	R

J

Name										

Entry 1

Name

Address	20__		20__		20__		20__		20__	
	S	R	S	R	S	R	S	R	S	R

	20__		20__		20__		20__		20__	
Email	S	R	S	R	S	R	S	R	S	R

Entry 2

Name

Address	20__		20__		20__		20__		20__	
	S	R	S	R	S	R	S	R	S	R

	20__		20__		20__		20__		20__	
Email	S	R	S	R	S	R	S	R	S	R

Entry 3

Name

Address	20__		20__		20__		20__		20__	
	S	R	S	R	S	R	S	R	S	R

	20__		20__		20__		20__		20__	
Email	S	R	S	R	S	R	S	R	S	R

Entry 4

Name

Address	20__		20__		20__		20__		20__	
	S	R	S	R	S	R	S	R	S	R

	20__		20__		20__		20__		20__	
Email	S	R	S	R	S	R	S	R	S	R

Entry 1

Name										
Address	20__		20__		20__		20__		20__	
	S	R	S	R	S	R	S	R	S	R
	20__		20__		20__		20__		20__	
Email	S	R	S	R	S	R	S	R	S	R

Entry 2

Name										
Address	20__		20__		20__		20__		20__	
	S	R	S	R	S	R	S	R	S	R
	20__		20__		20__		20__		20__	
Email	S	R	S	R	S	R	S	R	S	R

Entry 3

Name										
Address	20__		20__		20__		20__		20__	
	S	R	S	R	S	R	S	R	S	R
	20__		20__		20__		20__		20__	
Email	S	R	S	R	S	R	S	R	S	R

Entry 4

Name										
Address	20__		20__		20__		20__		20__	
	S	R	S	R	S	R	S	R	S	R
	20__		20__		20__		20__		20__	
Email	S	R	S	R	S	R	S	R	S	R

Name

Address

20__		20__		20__		20__		20__	
S	R	S	R	S	R	S	R	S	R

20__		20__		20__		20__		20__	
S	R	S	R	S	R	S	R	S	R

Email

Name

Address

20__		20__		20__		20__		20__	
S	R	S	R	S	R	S	R	S	R

20__		20__		20__		20__		20__	
S	R	S	R	S	R	S	R	S	R

Email

Name

Address

20__		20__		20__		20__		20__	
S	R	S	R	S	R	S	R	S	R

20__		20__		20__		20__		20__	
S	R	S	R	S	R	S	R	S	R

Email

Name

Address

20__		20__		20__		20__		20__	
S	R	S	R	S	R	S	R	S	R

20__		20__		20__		20__		20__	
S	R	S	R	S	R	S	R	S	R

Email

Name

Address	20__		20__		20__		20__		20__	
	S	R	S	R	S	R	S	R	S	R
	20__		20__		20__		20__		20__	
Email	S	R	S	R	S	R	S	R	S	R

Name

Address	20__		20__		20__		20__		20__	
	S	R	S	R	S	R	S	R	S	R
	20__		20__		20__		20__		20__	
Email	S	R	S	R	S	R	S	R	S	R

Name

Address	20__		20__		20__		20__		20__	
	S	R	S	R	S	R	S	R	S	R
	20__		20__		20__		20__		20__	
Email	S	R	S	R	S	R	S	R	S	R

Name

Address	20__		20__		20__		20__		20__	
	S	R	S	R	S	R	S	R	S	R
	20__		20__		20__		20__		20__	
Email	S	R	S	R	S	R	S	R	S	R

Name

Address	20__		20__		20__		20__		20__	
	S	R	S	R	S	R	S	R	S	R
	20__		20__		20__		20__		20__	
Email	S	R	S	R	S	R	S	R	S	R

Name

Address	20__		20__		20__		20__		20__	
	S	R	S	R	S	R	S	R	S	R
	20__		20__		20__		20__		20__	
Email	S	R	S	R	S	R	S	R	S	R

Name

Address	20__		20__		20__		20__		20__	
	S	R	S	R	S	R	S	R	S	R
	20__		20__		20__		20__		20__	
Email	S	R	S	R	S	R	S	R	S	R

Name

Address	20__		20__		20__		20__		20__	
	S	R	S	R	S	R	S	R	S	R
	20__		20__		20__		20__		20__	
Email	S	R	S	R	S	R	S	R	S	R

K

Name										

Address	20__		20__		20__		20__		20__	
	S	R	S	R	S	R	S	R	S	R
	20__		20__		20__		20__		20__	
Email	S	R	S	R	S	R	S	R	S	R

Name										

Address	20__		20__		20__		20__		20__	
	S	R	S	R	S	R	S	R	S	R
	20__		20__		20__		20__		20__	
Email	S	R	S	R	S	R	S	R	S	R

Name										

Address	20__		20__		20__		20__		20__	
	S	R	S	R	S	R	S	R	S	R
	20__		20__		20__		20__		20__	
Email	S	R	S	R	S	R	S	R	S	R

Name										

Address	20__		20__		20__		20__		20__	
	S	R	S	R	S	R	S	R	S	R
	20__		20__		20__		20__		20__	
Email	S	R	S	R	S	R	S	R	S	R

Name										
Address	20__		20__		20__		20__		20__	
	S	R	S	R	S	R	S	R	S	R
	20__		20__		20__		20__		20__	
Email	S	R	S	R	S	R	S	R	S	R

Name										
Address	20__		20__		20__		20__		20__	
	S	R	S	R	S	R	S	R	S	R
	20__		20__		20__		20__		20__	
Email	S	R	S	R	S	R	S	R	S	R

Name										
Address	20__		20__		20__		20__		20__	
	S	R	S	R	S	R	S	R	S	R
	20__		20__		20__		20__		20__	
Email	S	R	S	R	S	R	S	R	S	R

Name										
Address	20__		20__		20__		20__		20__	
	S	R	S	R	S	R	S	R	S	R
	20__		20__		20__		20__		20__	
Email	S	R	S	R	S	R	S	R	S	R

K

Name										
Address	20__		20__		20__		20__		20__	
	S	R	S	R	S	R	S	R	S	R
	20__		20__		20__		20__		20__	
Email	S	R	S	R	S	R	S	R	S	R

Name										
Address	20__		20__		20__		20__		20__	
	S	R	S	R	S	R	S	R	S	R
	20__		20__		20__		20__		20__	
Email	S	R	S	R	S	R	S	R	S	R

Name										
Address	20__		20__		20__		20__		20__	
	S	R	S	R	S	R	S	R	S	R
	20__		20__		20__		20__		20__	
Email	S	R	S	R	S	R	S	R	S	R

Name										
Address	20__		20__		20__		20__		20__	
	S	R	S	R	S	R	S	R	S	R
	20__		20__		20__		20__		20__	
Email	S	R	S	R	S	R	S	R	S	R

Name	Francis Long									
Address	33 Queenway	20**2~**		20__		20__		20__		20__
	Warminster	S	R	S	R	S	R	S	R	S	R
		✓									
		20__		20__		20__		20__		20__	
Email		S	R	S	R	S	R	S	R	S	R

Name										
Address	20__		20__		20__		20__		20__	
	S	R	S	R	S	R	S	R	S	R
	20__		20__		20__		20__		20__	
Email	S	R	S	R	S	R	S	R	S	R

Name										
Address	20__		20__		20__		20__		20__	
	S	R	S	R	S	R	S	R	S	R
	20__		20__		20__		20__		20__	
Email	S	R	S	R	S	R	S	R	S	R

Name										
Address	20__		20__		20__		20__		20__	
	S	R	S	R	S	R	S	R	S	R
	20__		20__		20__		20__		20__	
Email	S	R	S	R	S	R	S	R	S	R

L

Name

Address	20__		20__		20__		20__		20__	
	S	R	S	R	S	R	S	R	S	R
	20__		20__		20__		20__		20__	
	S	R	S	R	S	R	S	R	S	R
Email										

Name

Address	20__		20__		20__		20__		20__	
	S	R	S	R	S	R	S	R	S	R
	20__		20__		20__		20__		20__	
	S	R	S	R	S	R	S	R	S	R
Email										

Name

Address	20__		20__		20__		20__		20__	
	S	R	S	R	S	R	S	R	S	R
	20__		20__		20__		20__		20__	
	S	R	S	R	S	R	S	R	S	R
Email										

Name

Address	20__		20__		20__		20__		20__	
	S	R	S	R	S	R	S	R	S	R
	20__		20__		20__		20__		20__	
	S	R	S	R	S	R	S	R	S	R
Email										

Name

Address	20__		20__		20__		20__		20__	
	S	R	S	R	S	R	S	R	S	R
	20__		20__		20__		20__		20__	
Email	S	R	S	R	S	R	S	R	S	R

Name

Address	20__		20__		20__		20__		20__	
	S	R	S	R	S	R	S	R	S	R
	20__		20__		20__		20__		20__	
Email	S	R	S	R	S	R	S	R	S	R

Name

Address	20__		20__		20__		20__		20__	
	S	R	S	R	S	R	S	R	S	R
	20__		20__		20__		20__		20__	
Email	S	R	S	R	S	R	S	R	S	R

Name

Address	20__		20__		20__		20__		20__	
	S	R	S	R	S	R	S	R	S	R
	20__		20__		20__		20__		20__	
Email	S	R	S	R	S	R	S	R	S	R

L

Name										
Address	20__		20__		20__		20__		20__	
	S	R	S	R	S	R	S	R	S	R
	20__		20__		20__		20__		20__	
Email	S	R	S	R	S	R	S	R	S	R

Name										
Address	20__		20__		20__		20__		20__	
	S	R	S	R	S	R	S	R	S	R
	20__		20__		20__		20__		20__	
Email	S	R	S	R	S	R	S	R	S	R

Name										
Address	20__		20__		20__		20__		20__	
	S	R	S	R	S	R	S	R	S	R
	20__		20__		20__		20__		20__	
Email	S	R	S	R	S	R	S	R	S	R

Name										
Address	20__		20__		20__		20__		20__	
	S	R	S	R	S	R	S	R	S	R
	20__		20__		20__		20__		20__	
Email	S	R	S	R	S	R	S	R	S	R

Name

Address	20__		20__		20__		20__		20__	
	S	R	S	R	S	R	S	R	S	R
	20__		20__		20__		20__		20__	
Email	S	R	S	R	S	R	S	R	S	R

Name

Address	20__		20__		20__		20__		20__	
	S	R	S	R	S	R	S	R	S	R
	20__		20__		20__		20__		20__	
Email	S	R	S	R	S	R	S	R	S	R

Name

Address	20__		20__		20__		20__		20__	
	S	R	S	R	S	R	S	R	S	R
	20__		20__		20__		20__		20__	
Email	S	R	S	R	S	R	S	R	S	R

Name

Address	20__		20__		20__		20__		20__	
	S	R	S	R	S	R	S	R	S	R
	20__		20__		20__		20__		20__	
Email	S	R	S	R	S	R	S	R	S	R

L

Name										

Address	20__		20__		20__		20__		20__	
	S	R	S	R	S	R	S	R	S	R
	20__		20__		20__		20__		20__	
Email	S	R	S	R	S	R	S	R	S	R

Name										

Address	20__		20__		20__		20__		20__	
	S	R	S	R	S	R	S	R	S	R
	20__		20__		20__		20__		20__	
Email	S	R	S	R	S	R	S	R	S	R

Name										

Address	20__		20__		20__		20__		20__	
	S	R	S	R	S	R	S	R	S	R
	20__		20__		20__		20__		20__	
Email	S	R	S	R	S	R	S	R	S	R

Name										

Address	20__		20__		20__		20__		20__	
	S	R	S	R	S	R	S	R	S	R
	20__		20__		20__		20__		20__	
Email	S	R	S	R	S	R	S	R	S	R

Name

Address	20__		20__		20__		20__		20__	
	S	R	S	R	S	R	S	R	S	R
	20__		20__		20__		20__		20__	
Email	S	R	S	R	S	R	S	R	S	R

Name

Address	20__		20__		20__		20__		20__	
	S	R	S	R	S	R	S	R	S	R
	20__		20__		20__		20__		20__	
Email	S	R	S	R	S	R	S	R	S	R

Name

Address	20__		20__		20__		20__		20__	
	S	R	S	R	S	R	S	R	S	R
	20__		20__		20__		20__		20__	
Email	S	R	S	R	S	R	S	R	S	R

Name

Address	20__		20__		20__		20__		20__	
	S	R	S	R	S	R	S	R	S	R
	20__		20__		20__		20__		20__	
Email	S	R	S	R	S	R	S	R	S	R

M

Name

Address	20__		20__		20__		20__		20__	
	S	R	S	R	S	R	S	R	S	R
	20__		20__		20__		20__		20__	
Email	S	R	S	R	S	R	S	R	S	R

Name

Address	20__		20__		20__		20__		20__	
	S	R	S	R	S	R	S	R	S	R
	20__		20__		20__		20__		20__	
Email	S	R	S	R	S	R	S	R	S	R

Name

Address	20__		20__		20__		20__		20__	
	S	R	S	R	S	R	S	R	S	R
	20__		20__		20__		20__		20__	
Email	S	R	S	R	S	R	S	R	S	R

Name

Address	20__		20__		20__		20__		20__	
	S	R	S	R	S	R	S	R	S	R
	20__		20__		20__		20__		20__	
Email	S	R	S	R	S	R	S	R	S	R

Name

Address	20__		20__		20__		20__		20__	
	S	R	S	R	S	R	S	R	S	R
	20__		20__		20__		20__		20__	
	S	R	S	R	S	R	S	R	S	R
Email										

Name

Address	20__		20__		20__		20__		20__	
	S	R	S	R	S	R	S	R	S	R
	20__		20__		20__		20__		20__	
	S	R	S	R	S	R	S	R	S	R
Email										

Name

Address	20__		20__		20__		20__		20__	
	S	R	S	R	S	R	S	R	S	R
	20__		20__		20__		20__		20__	
	S	R	S	R	S	R	S	R	S	R
Email										

Name

Address	20__		20__		20__		20__		20__	
	S	R	S	R	S	R	S	R	S	R
	20__		20__		20__		20__		20__	
	S	R	S	R	S	R	S	R	S	R
Email										

M

Name

Address	20__		20__		20__		20__		20__	
	S	R	S	R	S	R	S	R	S	R
	20__		20__		20__		20__		20__	
Email	S	R	S	R	S	R	S	R	S	R

Name

Address	20__		20__		20__		20__		20__	
	S	R	S	R	S	R	S	R	S	R
	20__		20__		20__		20__		20__	
Email	S	R	S	R	S	R	S	R	S	R

Name

Address	20__		20__		20__		20__		20__	
	S	R	S	R	S	R	S	R	S	R
	20__		20__		20__		20__		20__	
Email	S	R	S	R	S	R	S	R	S	R

Name

Address	20__		20__		20__		20__		20__	
	S	R	S	R	S	R	S	R	S	R
	20__		20__		20__		20__		20__	
Email	S	R	S	R	S	R	S	R	S	R

Name

Address	20__		20__		20__		20__		20__	
	S	R	S	R	S	R	S	R	S	R
	20__		20__		20__		20__		20__	
Email	S	R	S	R	S	R	S	R	S	R

Name

Address	20__		20__		20__		20__		20__	
	S	R	S	R	S	R	S	R	S	R
	20__		20__		20__		20__		20__	
Email	S	R	S	R	S	R	S	R	S	R

Name

Address	20__		20__		20__		20__		20__	
	S	R	S	R	S	R	S	R	S	R
	20__		20__		20__		20__		20__	
Email	S	R	S	R	S	R	S	R	S	R

Name

Address	20__		20__		20__		20__		20__	
	S	R	S	R	S	R	S	R	S	R
	20__		20__		20__		20__		20__	
Email	S	R	S	R	S	R	S	R	S	R

M

Name

Address	20__		20__		20__		20__		20__	
	S	R	S	R	S	R	S	R	S	R
	20__		20__		20__		20__		20__	
Email	S	R	S	R	S	R	S	R	S	R

Name

Address	20__		20__		20__		20__		20__	
	S	R	S	R	S	R	S	R	S	R
	20__		20__		20__		20__		20__	
Email	S	R	S	R	S	R	S	R	S	R

Name

Address	20__		20__		20__		20__		20__	
	S	R	S	R	S	R	S	R	S	R
	20__		20__		20__		20__		20__	
Email	S	R	S	R	S	R	S	R	S	R

Name

Address	20__		20__		20__		20__		20__	
	S	R	S	R	S	R	S	R	S	R
	20__		20__		20__		20__		20__	
Email	S	R	S	R	S	R	S	R	S	R

Name

Address	20__		20__		20__		20__		20__	
	S	R	S	R	S	R	S	R	S	R
	20__		20__		20__		20__		20__	
Email	S	R	S	R	S	R	S	R	S	R

Name

Address	20__		20__		20__		20__		20__	
	S	R	S	R	S	R	S	R	S	R
	20__		20__		20__		20__		20__	
Email	S	R	S	R	S	R	S	R	S	R

Name

Address	20__		20__		20__		20__		20__	
	S	R	S	R	S	R	S	R	S	R
	20__		20__		20__		20__		20__	
Email	S	R	S	R	S	R	S	R	S	R

Name

Address	20__		20__		20__		20__		20__	
	S	R	S	R	S	R	S	R	S	R
	20__		20__		20__		20__		20__	
Email	S	R	S	R	S	R	S	R	S	R

Name

Address	20__		20__		20__		20__		20__	
	S	R	S	R	S	R	S	R	S	R
	20__		20__		20__		20__		20__	
Email	S	R	S	R	S	R	S	R	S	R

Name

Address	20__		20__		20__		20__		20__	
	S	R	S	R	S	R	S	R	S	R
	20__		20__		20__		20__		20__	
Email	S	R	S	R	S	R	S	R	S	R

Name

Address	20__		20__		20__		20__		20__	
	S	R	S	R	S	R	S	R	S	R
	20__		20__		20__		20__		20__	
Email	S	R	S	R	S	R	S	R	S	R

Name

Address	20__		20__		20__		20__		20__	
	S	R	S	R	S	R	S	R	S	R
	20__		20__		20__		20__		20__	
Email	S	R	S	R	S	R	S	R	S	R

Name										
Address	20__		20__		20__		20__		20__	
	S	R	S	R	S	R	S	R	S	R
	20__		20__		20__		20__		20__	
Email	S	R	S	R	S	R	S	R	S	R

Name										
Address	20__		20__		20__		20__		20__	
	S	R	S	R	S	R	S	R	S	R
	20__		20__		20__		20__		20__	
Email	S	R	S	R	S	R	S	R	S	R

Name										
Address	20__		20__		20__		20__		20__	
	S	R	S	R	S	R	S	R	S	R
	20__		20__		20__		20__		20__	
Email	S	R	S	R	S	R	S	R	S	R

Name										
Address	20__		20__		20__		20__		20__	
	S	R	S	R	S	R	S	R	S	R
	20__		20__		20__		20__		20__	
Email	S	R	S	R	S	R	S	R	S	R

N

Name

Address	20__		20__		20__		20__		20__	
	S	R	S	R	S	R	S	R	S	R
	20__		20__		20__		20__		20__	
Email	S	R	S	R	S	R	S	R	S	R

Name

Address	20__		20__		20__		20__		20__	
	S	R	S	R	S	R	S	R	S	R
	20__		20__		20__		20__		20__	
Email	S	R	S	R	S	R	S	R	S	R

Name

Address	20__		20__		20__		20__		20__	
	S	R	S	R	S	R	S	R	S	R
	20__		20__		20__		20__		20__	
Email	S	R	S	R	S	R	S	R	S	R

Name

Address	20__		20__		20__		20__		20__	
	S	R	S	R	S	R	S	R	S	R
	20__		20__		20__		20__		20__	
Email	S	R	S	R	S	R	S	R	S	R

Name										
Address	20__		20__		20__		20__		20__	
	S	R	S	R	S	R	S	R	S	R
	20__		20__		20__		20__		20__	
Email	S	R	S	R	S	R	S	R	S	R

Name										
Address	20__		20__		20__		20__		20__	
	S	R	S	R	S	R	S	R	S	R
	20__		20__		20__		20__		20__	
Email	S	R	S	R	S	R	S	R	S	R

Name										
Address	20__		20__		20__		20__		20__	
	S	R	S	R	S	R	S	R	S	R
	20__		20__		20__		20__		20__	
Email	S	R	S	R	S	R	S	R	S	R

Name										
Address	20__		20__		20__		20__		20__	
	S	R	S	R	S	R	S	R	S	R
	20__		20__		20__		20__		20__	
Email	S	R	S	R	S	R	S	R	S	R

N

Name

Address	20__		20__		20__		20__		20__	
	S	R	S	R	S	R	S	R	S	R
	20__		20__		20__		20__		20__	
Email	S	R	S	R	S	R	S	R	S	R

Name

Address	20__		20__		20__		20__		20__	
	S	R	S	R	S	R	S	R	S	R
	20__		20__		20__		20__		20__	
Email	S	R	S	R	S	R	S	R	S	R

Name

Address	20__		20__		20__		20__		20__	
	S	R	S	R	S	R	S	R	S	R
	20__		20__		20__		20__		20__	
Email	S	R	S	R	S	R	S	R	S	R

Name

Address	20__		20__		20__		20__		20__	
	S	R	S	R	S	R	S	R	S	R
	20__		20__		20__		20__		20__	
Email	S	R	S	R	S	R	S	R	S	R

○

Name										
Address	20__		20__		20__		20__		20__	
	S	R	S	R	S	R	S	R	S	R
	20__		20__		20__		20__		20__	
Email	S	R	S	R	S	R	S	R	S	R

Name										
Address	20__		20__		20__		20__		20__	
	S	R	S	R	S	R	S	R	S	R
	20__		20__		20__		20__		20__	
Email	S	R	S	R	S	R	S	R	S	R

Name										
Address	20__		20__		20__		20__		20__	
	S	R	S	R	S	R	S	R	S	R
	20__		20__		20__		20__		20__	
Email	S	R	S	R	S	R	S	R	S	R

Name										
Address	20__		20__		20__		20__		20__	
	S	R	S	R	S	R	S	R	S	R
	20__		20__		20__		20__		20__	
Email	S	R	S	R	S	R	S	R	S	R

○

Entry 1

Name

Address

20__		20__		20__		20__		20__	
S	R	S	R	S	R	S	R	S	R

20__		20__		20__		20__		20__	
S	R	S	R	S	R	S	R	S	R

Email

Entry 2

Name

Address

20__		20__		20__		20__		20__	
S	R	S	R	S	R	S	R	S	R

20__		20__		20__		20__		20__	
S	R	S	R	S	R	S	R	S	R

Email

Entry 3

Name

Address

20__		20__		20__		20__		20__	
S	R	S	R	S	R	S	R	S	R

20__		20__		20__		20__		20__	
S	R	S	R	S	R	S	R	S	R

Email

Entry 4

Name

Address

20__		20__		20__		20__		20__	
S	R	S	R	S	R	S	R	S	R

20__		20__		20__		20__		20__	
S	R	S	R	S	R	S	R	S	R

Email

○

Name										

Block 1

Address	20__		20__		20__		20__		20__	
	S	R	S	R	S	R	S	R	S	R
	20__		20__		20__		20__		20__	
Email	S	R	S	R	S	R	S	R	S	R

Name										

Block 2

Address	20__		20__		20__		20__		20__	
	S	R	S	R	S	R	S	R	S	R
	20__		20__		20__		20__		20__	
Email	S	R	S	R	S	R	S	R	S	R

Name										

Block 3

Address	20__		20__		20__		20__		20__	
	S	R	S	R	S	R	S	R	S	R
	20__		20__		20__		20__		20__	
Email	S	R	S	R	S	R	S	R	S	R

Name										

Block 4

Address	20__		20__		20__		20__		20__	
	S	R	S	R	S	R	S	R	S	R
	20__		20__		20__		20__		20__	
Email	S	R	S	R	S	R	S	R	S	R

◯

Name										
Address	20__		20__		20__		20__		20__	
	S	R	S	R	S	R	S	R	S	R
	20__		20__		20__		20__		20__	
Email	S	R	S	R	S	R	S	R	S	R

Name										
Address	20__		20__		20__		20__		20__	
	S	R	S	R	S	R	S	R	S	R
	20__		20__		20__		20__		20__	
Email	S	R	S	R	S	R	S	R	S	R

Name										
Address	20__		20__		20__		20__		20__	
	S	R	S	R	S	R	S	R	S	R
	20__		20__		20__		20__		20__	
Email	S	R	S	R	S	R	S	R	S	R

Name										
Address	20__		20__		20__		20__		20__	
	S	R	S	R	S	R	S	R	S	R
	20__		20__		20__		20__		20__	
Email	S	R	S	R	S	R	S	R	S	R

○

Name

Address	20__		20__		20__		20__		20__	
	S	R	S	R	S	R	S	R	S	R
	20__		20__		20__		20__		20__	
Email	S	R	S	R	S	R	S	R	S	R

Name

Address	20__		20__		20__		20__		20__	
	S	R	S	R	S	R	S	R	S	R
	20__		20__		20__		20__		20__	
Email	S	R	S	R	S	R	S	R	S	R

Name

Address	20__		20__		20__		20__		20__	
	S	R	S	R	S	R	S	R	S	R
	20__		20__		20__		20__		20__	
Email	S	R	S	R	S	R	S	R	S	R

Name

Address	20__		20__		20__		20__		20__	
	S	R	S	R	S	R	S	R	S	R
	20__		20__		20__		20__		20__	
Email	S	R	S	R	S	R	S	R	S	R

○

Name										
Address	20__		20__		20__		20__		20__	
	S	R	S	R	S	R	S	R	S	R
	20__		20__		20__		20__		20__	
Email	S	R	S	R	S	R	S	R	S	R

Name										
Address	20__		20__		20__		20__		20__	
	S	R	S	R	S	R	S	R	S	R
	20__		20__		20__		20__		20__	
Email	S	R	S	R	S	R	S	R	S	R

Name										
Address	20__		20__		20__		20__		20__	
	S	R	S	R	S	R	S	R	S	R
	20__		20__		20__		20__		20__	
Email	S	R	S	R	S	R	S	R	S	R

Name										
Address	20__		20__		20__		20__		20__	
	S	R	S	R	S	R	S	R	S	R
	20__		20__		20__		20__		20__	
Email	S	R	S	R	S	R	S	R	S	R

Name										

Address	20__		20__		20__		20__		20__	
	S	R	S	R	S	R	S	R	S	R

	20__		20__		20__		20__		20__	
Email	S	R	S	R	S	R	S	R	S	R

Name										

Address	20__		20__		20__		20__		20__	
	S	R	S	R	S	R	S	R	S	R

	20__		20__		20__		20__		20__	
Email	S	R	S	R	S	R	S	R	S	R

Name										

Address	20__		20__		20__		20__		20__	
	S	R	S	R	S	R	S	R	S	R

	20__		20__		20__		20__		20__	
Email	S	R	S	R	S	R	S	R	S	R

Name										

Address	20__		20__		20__		20__		20__	
	S	R	S	R	S	R	S	R	S	R

	20__		20__		20__		20__		20__	
Email	S	R	S	R	S	R	S	R	S	R

P

Name										
Address	20__		20__		20__		20__		20__	
	S	R	S	R	S	R	S	R	S	R
	20__		20__		20__		20__		20__	
Email	S	R	S	R	S	R	S	R	S	R

Name										
Address	20__		20__		20__		20__		20__	
	S	R	S	R	S	R	S	R	S	R
	20__		20__		20__		20__		20__	
Email	S	R	S	R	S	R	S	R	S	R

Name										
Address	20__		20__		20__		20__		20__	
	S	R	S	R	S	R	S	R	S	R
	20__		20__		20__		20__		20__	
Email	S	R	S	R	S	R	S	R	S	R

Name										
Address	20__		20__		20__		20__		20__	
	S	R	S	R	S	R	S	R	S	R
	20__		20__		20__		20__		20__	
Email	S	R	S	R	S	R	S	R	S	R

P

Name

Address	20__		20__		20__		20__		20__	
	S	R	S	R	S	R	S	R	S	R
	20__		20__		20__		20__		20__	
Email	S	R	S	R	S	R	S	R	S	R

Name

Address	20__		20__		20__		20__		20__	
	S	R	S	R	S	R	S	R	S	R
	20__		20__		20__		20__		20__	
Email	S	R	S	R	S	R	S	R	S	R

Name

Address	20__		20__		20__		20__		20__	
	S	R	S	R	S	R	S	R	S	R
	20__		20__		20__		20__		20__	
Email	S	R	S	R	S	R	S	R	S	R

Name

Address	20__		20__		20__		20__		20__	
	S	R	S	R	S	R	S	R	S	R
	20__		20__		20__		20__		20__	
Email	S	R	S	R	S	R	S	R	S	R

P

Name

Address	20__		20__		20__		20__		20__	
	S	R	S	R	S	R	S	R	S	R
	20__		20__		20__		20__		20__	
Email	S	R	S	R	S	R	S	R	S	R

Name

Address	20__		20__		20__		20__		20__	
	S	R	S	R	S	R	S	R	S	R
	20__		20__		20__		20__		20__	
Email	S	R	S	R	S	R	S	R	S	R

Name

Address	20__		20__		20__		20__		20__	
	S	R	S	R	S	R	S	R	S	R
	20__		20__		20__		20__		20__	
Email	S	R	S	R	S	R	S	R	S	R

Name

Address	20__		20__		20__		20__		20__	
	S	R	S	R	S	R	S	R	S	R
	20__		20__		20__		20__		20__	
Email	S	R	S	R	S	R	S	R	S	R

Name										
Address	20__		20__		20__		20__		20__	
	S	R	S	R	S	R	S	R	S	R
	20__		20__		20__		20__		20__	
Email	S	R	S	R	S	R	S	R	S	R

Name										
Address	20__		20__		20__		20__		20__	
	S	R	S	R	S	R	S	R	S	R
	20__		20__		20__		20__		20__	
Email	S	R	S	R	S	R	S	R	S	R

Name										
Address	20__		20__		20__		20__		20__	
	S	R	S	R	S	R	S	R	S	R
	20__		20__		20__		20__		20__	
Email	S	R	S	R	S	R	S	R	S	R

Name										
Address	20__		20__		20__		20__		20__	
	S	R	S	R	S	R	S	R	S	R
	20__		20__		20__		20__		20__	
Email	S	R	S	R	S	R	S	R	S	R

P

Name										
Address	20__		20__		20__		20__		20__	
	S	R	S	R	S	R	S	R	S	R
	20__		20__		20__		20__		20__	
Email	S	R	S	R	S	R	S	R	S	R

Name										
Address	20__		20__		20__		20__		20__	
	S	R	S	R	S	R	S	R	S	R
	20__		20__		20__		20__		20__	
Email	S	R	S	R	S	R	S	R	S	R

Name										
Address	20__		20__		20__		20__		20__	
	S	R	S	R	S	R	S	R	S	R
	20__		20__		20__		20__		20__	
Email	S	R	S	R	S	R	S	R	S	R

Name										
Address	20__		20__		20__		20__		20__	
	S	R	S	R	S	R	S	R	S	R
	20__		20__		20__		20__		20__	
Email	S	R	S	R	S	R	S	R	S	R

Q

Name										
Address	20__		20__		20__		20__		20__	
	S	R	S	R	S	R	S	R	S	R
	20__		20__		20__		20__		20__	
Email	S	R	S	R	S	R	S	R	S	R

Name										
Address	20__		20__		20__		20__		20__	
	S	R	S	R	S	R	S	R	S	R
	20__		20__		20__		20__		20__	
Email	S	R	S	R	S	R	S	R	S	R

Name										
Address	20__		20__		20__		20__		20__	
	S	R	S	R	S	R	S	R	S	R
	20__		20__		20__		20__		20__	
Email	S	R	S	R	S	R	S	R	S	R

Name										
Address	20__		20__		20__		20__		20__	
	S	R	S	R	S	R	S	R	S	R
	20__		20__		20__		20__		20__	
Email	S	R	S	R	S	R	S	R	S	R

Q

Name

Address	20__		20__		20__		20__		20__	
	S	R	S	R	S	R	S	R	S	R
	20__		20__		20__		20__		20__	
Email	S	R	S	R	S	R	S	R	S	R

Name

Address	20__		20__		20__		20__		20__	
	S	R	S	R	S	R	S	R	S	R
	20__		20__		20__		20__		20__	
Email	S	R	S	R	S	R	S	R	S	R

Name

Address	20__		20__		20__		20__		20__	
	S	R	S	R	S	R	S	R	S	R
	20__		20__		20__		20__		20__	
Email	S	R	S	R	S	R	S	R	S	R

Name

Address	20__		20__		20__		20__		20__	
	S	R	S	R	S	R	S	R	S	R
	20__		20__		20__		20__		20__	
Email	S	R	S	R	S	R	S	R	S	R

Q

Name										

Block 1

Address	20__		20__		20__		20__		20__	
	S	R	S	R	S	R	S	R	S	R
	20__		20__		20__		20__		20__	
Email	S	R	S	R	S	R	S	R	S	R

Block 2

Address	20__		20__		20__		20__		20__	
	S	R	S	R	S	R	S	R	S	R
	20__		20__		20__		20__		20__	
Email	S	R	S	R	S	R	S	R	S	R

Block 3

Address	20__		20__		20__		20__		20__	
	S	R	S	R	S	R	S	R	S	R
	20__		20__		20__		20__		20__	
Email	S	R	S	R	S	R	S	R	S	R

Block 4

Address	20__		20__		20__		20__		20__	
	S	R	S	R	S	R	S	R	S	R
	20__		20__		20__		20__		20__	
Email	S	R	S	R	S	R	S	R	S	R

Q

Name

Address	20__		20__		20__		20__		20__	
	S	R	S	R	S	R	S	R	S	R
	20__		20__		20__		20__		20__	
Email	S	R	S	R	S	R	S	R	S	R

Name

Address	20__		20__		20__		20__		20__	
	S	R	S	R	S	R	S	R	S	R
	20__		20__		20__		20__		20__	
Email	S	R	S	R	S	R	S	R	S	R

Name

Address	20__		20__		20__		20__		20__	
	S	R	S	R	S	R	S	R	S	R
	20__		20__		20__		20__		20__	
Email	S	R	S	R	S	R	S	R	S	R

Name

Address	20__		20__		20__		20__		20__	
	S	R	S	R	S	R	S	R	S	R
	20__		20__		20__		20__		20__	
Email	S	R	S	R	S	R	S	R	S	R

Q

Name										

Address	20__		20__		20__		20__		20__	
	S	R	S	R	S	R	S	R	S	R
	20__		20__		20__		20__		20__	
Email	S	R	S	R	S	R	S	R	S	R

Name										

Address	20__		20__		20__		20__		20__	
	S	R	S	R	S	R	S	R	S	R
	20__		20__		20__		20__		20__	
Email	S	R	S	R	S	R	S	R	S	R

Name										

Address	20__		20__		20__		20__		20__	
	S	R	S	R	S	R	S	R	S	R
	20__		20__		20__		20__		20__	
Email	S	R	S	R	S	R	S	R	S	R

Name										

Address	20__		20__		20__		20__		20__	
	S	R	S	R	S	R	S	R	S	R
	20__		20__		20__		20__		20__	
Email	S	R	S	R	S	R	S	R	S	R

Q

Name

Address	20__		20__		20__		20__		20__	
	S	R	S	R	S	R	S	R	S	R
	20__		20__		20__		20__		20__	
Email	S	R	S	R	S	R	S	R	S	R

Name

Address	20__		20__		20__		20__		20__	
	S	R	S	R	S	R	S	R	S	R
	20__		20__		20__		20__		20__	
Email	S	R	S	R	S	R	S	R	S	R

Name

Address	20__		20__		20__		20__		20__	
	S	R	S	R	S	R	S	R	S	R
	20__		20__		20__		20__		20__	
Email	S	R	S	R	S	R	S	R	S	R

Name

Address	20__		20__		20__		20__		20__	
	S	R	S	R	S	R	S	R	S	R
	20__		20__		20__		20__		20__	
Email	S	R	S	R	S	R	S	R	S	R

Name Dave Rowles

Address	20_2_2_		20__		20__		20__		20__	
	S	R	S	R	S	R	S	R	S	R
	20__		20__		20__		20__		20__	
Email	S	R	S	R	S	R	S	R	S	R

Name

Address	20__		20__		20__		20__		20__	
	S	R	S	R	S	R	S	R	S	R
	20__		20__		20__		20__		20__	
Email	S	R	S	R	S	R	S	R	S	R

Name

Address	20__		20__		20__		20__		20__	
	S	R	S	R	S	R	S	R	S	R
	20__		20__		20__		20__		20__	
Email	S	R	S	R	S	R	S	R	S	R

Name

Address	20__		20__		20__		20__		20__	
	S	R	S	R	S	R	S	R	S	R
	20__		20__		20__		20__		20__	
Email	S	R	S	R	S	R	S	R	S	R

R

Name						

Address	20__	20__	20__	20__	20__
	S	R	S	R	S	R	S	R	S	R
	20__	20__	20__	20__	20__
Email	S	R	S	R	S	R	S	R	S	R

Name						

Address	20__	20__	20__	20__	20__
	S	R	S	R	S	R	S	R	S	R
	20__	20__	20__	20__	20__
Email	S	R	S	R	S	R	S	R	S	R

Name						

Address	20__	20__	20__	20__	20__
	S	R	S	R	S	R	S	R	S	R
	20__	20__	20__	20__	20__
Email	S	R	S	R	S	R	S	R	S	R

Name						

Address	20__	20__	20__	20__	20__
	S	R	S	R	S	R	S	R	S	R
	20__	20__	20__	20__	20__
Email	S	R	S	R	S	R	S	R	S	R

R

Name										
Address	20__		20__		20__		20__		20__	
	S	R	S	R	S	R	S	R	S	R
	20__		20__		20__		20__		20__	
Email	S	R	S	R	S	R	S	R	S	R

Name										
Address	20__		20__		20__		20__		20__	
	S	R	S	R	S	R	S	R	S	R
	20__		20__		20__		20__		20__	
Email	S	R	S	R	S	R	S	R	S	R

Name										
Address	20__		20__		20__		20__		20__	
	S	R	S	R	S	R	S	R	S	R
	20__		20__		20__		20__		20__	
Email	S	R	S	R	S	R	S	R	S	R

Name										
Address	20__		20__		20__		20__		20__	
	S	R	S	R	S	R	S	R	S	R
	20__		20__		20__		20__		20__	
Email	S	R	S	R	S	R	S	R	S	R

R

Name										
Address	20__		20__		20__		20__		20__	
	S	R	S	R	S	R	S	R	S	R
	20__		20__		20__		20__		20__	
Email	S	R	S	R	S	R	S	R	S	R

Name										
Address	20__		20__		20__		20__		20__	
	S	R	S	R	S	R	S	R	S	R
	20__		20__		20__		20__		20__	
Email	S	R	S	R	S	R	S	R	S	R

Name										
Address	20__		20__		20__		20__		20__	
	S	R	S	R	S	R	S	R	S	R
	20__		20__		20__		20__		20__	
Email	S	R	S	R	S	R	S	R	S	R

Name										
Address	20__		20__		20__		20__		20__	
	S	R	S	R	S	R	S	R	S	R
	20__		20__		20__		20__		20__	
Email	S	R	S	R	S	R	S	R	S	R

Name										
Address	20__		20__		20__		20__		20__	
	S	R	S	R	S	R	S	R	S	R
	20__		20__		20__		20__		20__	
Email	S	R	S	R	S	R	S	R	S	R

Name										
Address	20__		20__		20__		20__		20__	
	S	R	S	R	S	R	S	R	S	R
	20__		20__		20__		20__		20__	
Email	S	R	S	R	S	R	S	R	S	R

Name										
Address	20__		20__		20__		20__		20__	
	S	R	S	R	S	R	S	R	S	R
	20__		20__		20__		20__		20__	
Email	S	R	S	R	S	R	S	R	S	R

Name										
Address	20__		20__		20__		20__		20__	
	S	R	S	R	S	R	S	R	S	R
	20__		20__		20__		20__		20__	
Email	S	R	S	R	S	R	S	R	S	R

R

Name										
Address	20__		20__		20__		20__		20__	
	S	R	S	R	S	R	S	R	S	R
	20__		20__		20__		20__		20__	
Email	S	R	S	R	S	R	S	R	S	R

Name										
Address	20__		20__		20__		20__		20__	
	S	R	S	R	S	R	S	R	S	R
	20__		20__		20__		20__		20__	
Email	S	R	S	R	S	R	S	R	S	R

Name										
Address	20__		20__		20__		20__		20__	
	S	R	S	R	S	R	S	R	S	R
	20__		20__		20__		20__		20__	
Email	S	R	S	R	S	R	S	R	S	R

Name										
Address	20__		20__		20__		20__		20__	
	S	R	S	R	S	R	S	R	S	R
	20__		20__		20__		20__		20__	
Email	S	R	S	R	S	R	S	R	S	R

S

| Name | Shirley | | | | | | | | | |

Address	20**21**		20__		20__		20__		20__	
	S	R	S	R	S	R	S	R	S	R
	20__		20__		20__		20__		20__	
Email	S	R	S	R	S	R	S	R	S	R

| Name | | | | | | | | | | |

Address	20__		20__		20__		20__		20__	
	S	R	S	R	S	R	S	R	S	R
	20__		20__		20__		20__		20__	
Email	S	R	S	R	S	R	S	R	S	R

| Name | | | | | | | | | | |

Address	20__		20__		20__		20__		20__	
	S	R	S	R	S	R	S	R	S	R
	20__		20__		20__		20__		20__	
Email	S	R	S	R	S	R	S	R	S	R

| Name | | | | | | | | | | |

Address	20__		20__		20__		20__		20__	
	S	R	S	R	S	R	S	R	S	R
	20__		20__		20__		20__		20__	
Email	S	R	S	R	S	R	S	R	S	R

S

Name

Address	20__		20__		20__		20__		20__	
	S	R	S	R	S	R	S	R	S	R
	20__		20__		20__		20__		20__	
Email	S	R	S	R	S	R	S	R	S	R

Name

Address	20__		20__		20__		20__		20__	
	S	R	S	R	S	R	S	R	S	R
	20__		20__		20__		20__		20__	
Email	S	R	S	R	S	R	S	R	S	R

Name

Address	20__		20__		20__		20__		20__	
	S	R	S	R	S	R	S	R	S	R
	20__		20__		20__		20__		20__	
Email	S	R	S	R	S	R	S	R	S	R

Name

Address	20__		20__		20__		20__		20__	
	S	R	S	R	S	R	S	R	S	R
	20__		20__		20__		20__		20__	
Email	S	R	S	R	S	R	S	R	S	R

Name

Address	20__		20__		20__		20__		20__	
	S	R	S	R	S	R	S	R	S	R
	20__		20__		20__		20__		20__	
Email	S	R	S	R	S	R	S	R	S	R

Name

Address	20__		20__		20__		20__		20__	
	S	R	S	R	S	R	S	R	S	R
	20__		20__		20__		20__		20__	
Email	S	R	S	R	S	R	S	R	S	R

Name

Address	20__		20__		20__		20__		20__	
	S	R	S	R	S	R	S	R	S	R
	20__		20__		20__		20__		20__	
Email	S	R	S	R	S	R	S	R	S	R

Name

Address	20__		20__		20__		20__		20__	
	S	R	S	R	S	R	S	R	S	R
	20__		20__		20__		20__		20__	
Email	S	R	S	R	S	R	S	R	S	R

S

Name

Address	20__		20__		20__		20__		20__	
	S	R	S	R	S	R	S	R	S	R
	20__		20__		20__		20__		20__	
Email	S	R	S	R	S	R	S	R	S	R

Name

Address	20__		20__		20__		20__		20__	
	S	R	S	R	S	R	S	R	S	R
	20__		20__		20__		20__		20__	
Email	S	R	S	R	S	R	S	R	S	R

Name

Address	20__		20__		20__		20__		20__	
	S	R	S	R	S	R	S	R	S	R
	20__		20__		20__		20__		20__	
Email	S	R	S	R	S	R	S	R	S	R

Name

Address	20__		20__		20__		20__		20__	
	S	R	S	R	S	R	S	R	S	R
	20__		20__		20__		20__		20__	
Email	S	R	S	R	S	R	S	R	S	R

S

Name										
Address	20__		20__		20__		20__		20__	
	S	R	S	R	S	R	S	R	S	R
	20__		20__		20__		20__		20__	
Email	S	R	S	R	S	R	S	R	S	R

Name										
Address	20__		20__		20__		20__		20__	
	S	R	S	R	S	R	S	R	S	R
	20__		20__		20__		20__		20__	
Email	S	R	S	R	S	R	S	R	S	R

Name										
Address	20__		20__		20__		20__		20__	
	S	R	S	R	S	R	S	R	S	R
	20__		20__		20__		20__		20__	
Email	S	R	S	R	S	R	S	R	S	R

Name										
Address	20__		20__		20__		20__		20__	
	S	R	S	R	S	R	S	R	S	R
	20__		20__		20__		20__		20__	
Email	S	R	S	R	S	R	S	R	S	R

S

Name

Address	20__		20__		20__		20__		20__	
	S	R	S	R	S	R	S	R	S	R
	20__		20__		20__		20__		20__	
Email	S	R	S	R	S	R	S	R	S	R

Name

Address	20__		20__		20__		20__		20__	
	S	R	S	R	S	R	S	R	S	R
	20__		20__		20__		20__		20__	
Email	S	R	S	R	S	R	S	R	S	R

Name

Address	20__		20__		20__		20__		20__	
	S	R	S	R	S	R	S	R	S	R
	20__		20__		20__		20__		20__	
Email	S	R	S	R	S	R	S	R	S	R

Name

Address	20__		20__		20__		20__		20__	
	S	R	S	R	S	R	S	R	S	R
	20__		20__		20__		20__		20__	
Email	S	R	S	R	S	R	S	R	S	R

Name										

Address

	20__		20__		20__		20__		20__	
	S	R	S	R	S	R	S	R	S	R

	20__		20__		20__		20__		20__	
Email	S	R	S	R	S	R	S	R	S	R

Name										

Address

	20__		20__		20__		20__		20__	
	S	R	S	R	S	R	S	R	S	R

	20__		20__		20__		20__		20__	
Email	S	R	S	R	S	R	S	R	S	R

Name										

Address

	20__		20__		20__		20__		20__	
	S	R	S	R	S	R	S	R	S	R

	20__		20__		20__		20__		20__	
Email	S	R	S	R	S	R	S	R	S	R

Name										

Address

	20__		20__		20__		20__		20__	
	S	R	S	R	S	R	S	R	S	R

	20__		20__		20__		20__		20__	
Email	S	R	S	R	S	R	S	R	S	R

T

Name					
Address	20__	20__	20__	20__	20__
	S R	S R	S R	S R	S R
	20__	20__	20__	20__	20__
Email	S R	S R	S R	S R	S R

Name					
Address	20__	20__	20__	20__	20__
	S R	S R	S R	S R	S R
	20__	20__	20__	20__	20__
Email	S R	S R	S R	S R	S R

Name					
Address	20__	20__	20__	20__	20__
	S R	S R	S R	S R	S R
	20__	20__	20__	20__	20__
Email	S R	S R	S R	S R	S R

Name					
Address	20__	20__	20__	20__	20__
	S R	S R	S R	S R	S R
	20__	20__	20__	20__	20__
Email	S R	S R	S R	S R	S R

Name										

Address	20__		20__		20__		20__		20__	
	S	R	S	R	S	R	S	R	S	R
	20__		20__		20__		20__		20__	
Email	S	R	S	R	S	R	S	R	S	R

Name										

Address	20__		20__		20__		20__		20__	
	S	R	S	R	S	R	S	R	S	R
	20__		20__		20__		20__		20__	
Email	S	R	S	R	S	R	S	R	S	R

Name										

Address	20__		20__		20__		20__		20__	
	S	R	S	R	S	R	S	R	S	R
	20__		20__		20__		20__		20__	
Email	S	R	S	R	S	R	S	R	S	R

Name										

Address	20__		20__		20__		20__		20__	
	S	R	S	R	S	R	S	R	S	R
	20__		20__		20__		20__		20__	
Email	S	R	S	R	S	R	S	R	S	R

T

Name					

Address	20__	20__	20__	20__	20__
	S | R	S | R	S | R	S | R	S | R
	20__	20__	20__	20__	20__
Email	S | R	S | R	S | R	S | R	S | R

Name					

Address	20__	20__	20__	20__	20__
	S | R	S | R	S | R	S | R	S | R
	20__	20__	20__	20__	20__
Email	S | R	S | R	S | R	S | R	S | R

Name					

Address	20__	20__	20__	20__	20__
	S | R	S | R	S | R	S | R	S | R
	20__	20__	20__	20__	20__
Email	S | R	S | R	S | R	S | R	S | R

Name					

Address	20__	20__	20__	20__	20__
	S | R	S | R	S | R	S | R	S | R
	20__	20__	20__	20__	20__
Email	S | R	S | R	S | R	S | R	S | R

Name										
Address	20__		20__		20__		20__		20__	
	S	R	S	R	S	R	S	R	S	R
	20__		20__		20__		20__		20__	
Email	S	R	S	R	S	R	S	R	S	R

Name										
Address	20__		20__		20__		20__		20__	
	S	R	S	R	S	R	S	R	S	R
	20__		20__		20__		20__		20__	
Email	S	R	S	R	S	R	S	R	S	R

Name										
Address	20__		20__		20__		20__		20__	
	S	R	S	R	S	R	S	R	S	R
	20__		20__		20__		20__		20__	
Email	S	R	S	R	S	R	S	R	S	R

Name										
Address	20__		20__		20__		20__		20__	
	S	R	S	R	S	R	S	R	S	R
	20__		20__		20__		20__		20__	
Email	S	R	S	R	S	R	S	R	S	R

T

Name

Address	20__		20__		20__		20__		20__	
	S	R	S	R	S	R	S	R	S	R
	20__		20__		20__		20__		20__	
Email	S	R	S	R	S	R	S	R	S	R

Name

Address	20__		20__		20__		20__		20__	
	S	R	S	R	S	R	S	R	S	R
	20__		20__		20__		20__		20__	
Email	S	R	S	R	S	R	S	R	S	R

Name

Address	20__		20__		20__		20__		20__	
	S	R	S	R	S	R	S	R	S	R
	20__		20__		20__		20__		20__	
Email	S	R	S	R	S	R	S	R	S	R

Name

Address	20__		20__		20__		20__		20__	
	S	R	S	R	S	R	S	R	S	R
	20__		20__		20__		20__		20__	
Email	S	R	S	R	S	R	S	R	S	R

Name

Address	20__		20__		20__		20__		20__	
	S	R	S	R	S	R	S	R	S	R
	20__		20__		20__		20__		20__	
Email	S	R	S	R	S	R	S	R	S	R

Name

Address	20__		20__		20__		20__		20__	
	S	R	S	R	S	R	S	R	S	R
	20__		20__		20__		20__		20__	
Email	S	R	S	R	S	R	S	R	S	R

Name

Address	20__		20__		20__		20__		20__	
	S	R	S	R	S	R	S	R	S	R
	20__		20__		20__		20__		20__	
Email	S	R	S	R	S	R	S	R	S	R

Name

Address	20__		20__		20__		20__		20__	
	S	R	S	R	S	R	S	R	S	R
	20__		20__		20__		20__		20__	
Email	S	R	S	R	S	R	S	R	S	R

U

Name										
Address	20__		20__		20__		20__		20__	
	S	R	S	R	S	R	S	R	S	R
	20__		20__		20__		20__		20__	
Email	S	R	S	R	S	R	S	R	S	R

Name										
Address	20__		20__		20__		20__		20__	
	S	R	S	R	S	R	S	R	S	R
	20__		20__		20__		20__		20__	
Email	S	R	S	R	S	R	S	R	S	R

Name										
Address	20__		20__		20__		20__		20__	
	S	R	S	R	S	R	S	R	S	R
	20__		20__		20__		20__		20__	
Email	S	R	S	R	S	R	S	R	S	R

Name										
Address	20__		20__		20__		20__		20__	
	S	R	S	R	S	R	S	R	S	R
	20__		20__		20__		20__		20__	
Email	S	R	S	R	S	R	S	R	S	R

Name										

Address	20__		20__		20__		20__		20__	
	S	R	S	R	S	R	S	R	S	R
	20__		20__		20__		20__		20__	
Email	S	R	S	R	S	R	S	R	S	R

Name										

Address	20__		20__		20__		20__		20__	
	S	R	S	R	S	R	S	R	S	R
	20__		20__		20__		20__		20__	
Email	S	R	S	R	S	R	S	R	S	R

Name										

Address	20__		20__		20__		20__		20__	
	S	R	S	R	S	R	S	R	S	R
	20__		20__		20__		20__		20__	
Email	S	R	S	R	S	R	S	R	S	R

Name										

Address	20__		20__		20__		20__		20__	
	S	R	S	R	S	R	S	R	S	R
	20__		20__		20__		20__		20__	
Email	S	R	S	R	S	R	S	R	S	R

U

Name										

Address	20__		20__		20__		20__		20__	
	S	R	S	R	S	R	S	R	S	R
	20__		20__		20__		20__		20__	
Email	S	R	S	R	S	R	S	R	S	R

Name										

Address	20__		20__		20__		20__		20__	
	S	R	S	R	S	R	S	R	S	R
	20__		20__		20__		20__		20__	
Email	S	R	S	R	S	R	S	R	S	R

Name										

Address	20__		20__		20__		20__		20__	
	S	R	S	R	S	R	S	R	S	R
	20__		20__		20__		20__		20__	
Email	S	R	S	R	S	R	S	R	S	R

Name										

Address	20__		20__		20__		20__		20__	
	S	R	S	R	S	R	S	R	S	R
	20__		20__		20__		20__		20__	
Email	S	R	S	R	S	R	S	R	S	R

U

Name										

Name (block 1)

Address	20__		20__		20__		20__		20__	
	S	R	S	R	S	R	S	R	S	R
	20__		20__		20__		20__		20__	
Email	S	R	S	R	S	R	S	R	S	R

Name (block 2)

Address	20__		20__		20__		20__		20__	
	S	R	S	R	S	R	S	R	S	R
	20__		20__		20__		20__		20__	
Email	S	R	S	R	S	R	S	R	S	R

Name (block 3)

Address	20__		20__		20__		20__		20__	
	S	R	S	R	S	R	S	R	S	R
	20__		20__		20__		20__		20__	
Email	S	R	S	R	S	R	S	R	S	R

Name (block 4)

Address	20__		20__		20__		20__		20__	
	S	R	S	R	S	R	S	R	S	R
	20__		20__		20__		20__		20__	
Email	S	R	S	R	S	R	S	R	S	R

Name										

Address	20__		20__		20__		20__		20__	
	S	R	S	R	S	R	S	R	S	R
	20__		20__		20__		20__		20__	
Email	S	R	S	R	S	R	S	R	S	R

Name										

Address	20__		20__		20__		20__		20__	
	S	R	S	R	S	R	S	R	S	R
	20__		20__		20__		20__		20__	
Email	S	R	S	R	S	R	S	R	S	R

Name										

Address	20__		20__		20__		20__		20__	
	S	R	S	R	S	R	S	R	S	R
	20__		20__		20__		20__		20__	
Email	S	R	S	R	S	R	S	R	S	R

Name										

Address	20__		20__		20__		20__		20__	
	S	R	S	R	S	R	S	R	S	R
	20__		20__		20__		20__		20__	
Email	S	R	S	R	S	R	S	R	S	R

V

Name

Address	20__		20__		20__		20__		20__	
	S	R	S	R	S	R	S	R	S	R
	20__		20__		20__		20__		20__	
Email	S	R	S	R	S	R	S	R	S	R

Name

Address	20__		20__		20__		20__		20__	
	S	R	S	R	S	R	S	R	S	R
	20__		20__		20__		20__		20__	
Email	S	R	S	R	S	R	S	R	S	R

Name

Address	20__		20__		20__		20__		20__	
	S	R	S	R	S	R	S	R	S	R
	20__		20__		20__		20__		20__	
Email	S	R	S	R	S	R	S	R	S	R

Name

Address	20__		20__		20__		20__		20__	
	S	R	S	R	S	R	S	R	S	R
	20__		20__		20__		20__		20__	
Email	S	R	S	R	S	R	S	R	S	R

V

Name

Address	20__		20__		20__		20__		20__	
	S	R	S	R	S	R	S	R	S	R
	20__		20__		20__		20__		20__	
Email	S	R	S	R	S	R	S	R	S	R

Name

Address	20__		20__		20__		20__		20__	
	S	R	S	R	S	R	S	R	S	R
	20__		20__		20__		20__		20__	
Email	S	R	S	R	S	R	S	R	S	R

Name

Address	20__		20__		20__		20__		20__	
	S	R	S	R	S	R	S	R	S	R
	20__		20__		20__		20__		20__	
Email	S	R	S	R	S	R	S	R	S	R

Name

Address	20__		20__		20__		20__		20__	
	S	R	S	R	S	R	S	R	S	R
	20__		20__		20__		20__		20__	
Email	S	R	S	R	S	R	S	R	S	R

Name										

Name

Address	20__		20__		20__		20__		20__	
	S	R	S	R	S	R	S	R	S	R
	20__		20__		20__		20__		20__	
Email	S	R	S	R	S	R	S	R	S	R

Name

Address	20__		20__		20__		20__		20__	
	S	R	S	R	S	R	S	R	S	R
	20__		20__		20__		20__		20__	
Email	S	R	S	R	S	R	S	R	S	R

Name

Address	20__		20__		20__		20__		20__	
	S	R	S	R	S	R	S	R	S	R
	20__		20__		20__		20__		20__	
Email	S	R	S	R	S	R	S	R	S	R

Name

Address	20__		20__		20__		20__		20__	
	S	R	S	R	S	R	S	R	S	R
	20__		20__		20__		20__		20__	
Email	S	R	S	R	S	R	S	R	S	R

	V

Name

Address	20__		20__		20__		20__		20__	
	S	R	S	R	S	R	S	R	S	R
	20__		20__		20__		20__		20__	
Email	S	R	S	R	S	R	S	R	S	R

Name

Address	20__		20__		20__		20__		20__	
	S	R	S	R	S	R	S	R	S	R
	20__		20__		20__		20__		20__	
Email	S	R	S	R	S	R	S	R	S	R

Name

Address	20__		20__		20__		20__		20__	
	S	R	S	R	S	R	S	R	S	R
	20__		20__		20__		20__		20__	
Email	S	R	S	R	S	R	S	R	S	R

Name

Address	20__		20__		20__		20__		20__	
	S	R	S	R	S	R	S	R	S	R
	20__		20__		20__		20__		20__	
Email	S	R	S	R	S	R	S	R	S	R

Name

Address	20__		20__		20__		20__		20__	
	S	R	S	R	S	R	S	R	S	R
	20__		20__		20__		20__		20__	
Email	S	R	S	R	S	R	S	R	S	R

Name

Address	20__		20__		20__		20__		20__	
	S	R	S	R	S	R	S	R	S	R
	20__		20__		20__		20__		20__	
Email	S	R	S	R	S	R	S	R	S	R

Name

Address	20__		20__		20__		20__		20__	
	S	R	S	R	S	R	S	R	S	R
	20__		20__		20__		20__		20__	
Email	S	R	S	R	S	R	S	R	S	R

Name

Address	20__		20__		20__		20__		20__	
	S	R	S	R	S	R	S	R	S	R
	20__		20__		20__		20__		20__	
Email	S	R	S	R	S	R	S	R	S	R

Name

Address	20__		20__		20__		20__		20__	
	S	R	S	R	S	R	S	R	S	R
	20__		20__		20__		20__		20__	
Email	S	R	S	R	S	R	S	R	S	R

Name

Address	20__		20__		20__		20__		20__	
	S	R	S	R	S	R	S	R	S	R
	20__		20__		20__		20__		20__	
Email	S	R	S	R	S	R	S	R	S	R

Name

Address	20__		20__		20__		20__		20__	
	S	R	S	R	S	R	S	R	S	R
	20__		20__		20__		20__		20__	
Email	S	R	S	R	S	R	S	R	S	R

Name

Address	20__		20__		20__		20__		20__	
	S	R	S	R	S	R	S	R	S	R
	20__		20__		20__		20__		20__	
Email	S	R	S	R	S	R	S	R	S	R

W

Name										
Address	20__		20__		20__		20__		20__	
	S	R	S	R	S	R	S	R	S	R
	20__		20__		20__		20__		20__	
Email	S	R	S	R	S	R	S	R	S	R

Name										
Address	20__		20__		20__		20__		20__	
	S	R	S	R	S	R	S	R	S	R
	20__		20__		20__		20__		20__	
Email	S	R	S	R	S	R	S	R	S	R

Name										
Address	20__		20__		20__		20__		20__	
	S	R	S	R	S	R	S	R	S	R
	20__		20__		20__		20__		20__	
Email	S	R	S	R	S	R	S	R	S	R

Name										
Address	20__		20__		20__		20__		20__	
	S	R	S	R	S	R	S	R	S	R
	20__		20__		20__		20__		20__	
Email	S	R	S	R	S	R	S	R	S	R

W

Name

Address	20__		20__		20__		20__		20__	
	S	R	S	R	S	R	S	R	S	R
	20__		20__		20__		20__		20__	
	S	R	S	R	S	R	S	R	S	R
Email										

Name

Address	20__		20__		20__		20__		20__	
	S	R	S	R	S	R	S	R	S	R
	20__		20__		20__		20__		20__	
	S	R	S	R	S	R	S	R	S	R
Email										

Name

Address	20__		20__		20__		20__		20__	
	S	R	S	R	S	R	S	R	S	R
	20__		20__		20__		20__		20__	
	S	R	S	R	S	R	S	R	S	R
Email										

Name

Address	20__		20__		20__		20__		20__	
	S	R	S	R	S	R	S	R	S	R
	20__		20__		20__		20__		20__	
	S	R	S	R	S	R	S	R	S	R
Email										

W

Name										

Address	20__		20__		20__		20__		20__	
	S	R	S	R	S	R	S	R	S	R

	20__		20__		20__		20__		20__	
Email	S	R	S	R	S	R	S	R	S	R

Name										

Address	20__		20__		20__		20__		20__	
	S	R	S	R	S	R	S	R	S	R

	20__		20__		20__		20__		20__	
Email	S	R	S	R	S	R	S	R	S	R

Name										

Address	20__		20__		20__		20__		20__	
	S	R	S	R	S	R	S	R	S	R

	20__		20__		20__		20__		20__	
Email	S	R	S	R	S	R	S	R	S	R

Name										

Address	20__		20__		20__		20__		20__	
	S	R	S	R	S	R	S	R	S	R

	20__		20__		20__		20__		20__	
Email	S	R	S	R	S	R	S	R	S	R

W

Name

Address	20__		20__		20__		20__		20__	
	S	R	S	R	S	R	S	R	S	R
	20__		20__		20__		20__		20__	
Email	S	R	S	R	S	R	S	R	S	R

Name

Address	20__		20__		20__		20__		20__	
	S	R	S	R	S	R	S	R	S	R
	20__		20__		20__		20__		20__	
Email	S	R	S	R	S	R	S	R	S	R

Name

Address	20__		20__		20__		20__		20__	
	S	R	S	R	S	R	S	R	S	R
	20__		20__		20__		20__		20__	
Email	S	R	S	R	S	R	S	R	S	R

Name

Address	20__		20__		20__		20__		20__	
	S	R	S	R	S	R	S	R	S	R
	20__		20__		20__		20__		20__	
Email	S	R	S	R	S	R	S	R	S	R

W

Name										

Section 1

Address	20__		20__		20__		20__		20__	
	S	R	S	R	S	R	S	R	S	R
	20__		20__		20__		20__		20__	
Email	S	R	S	R	S	R	S	R	S	R

Section 2

Address	20__		20__		20__		20__		20__	
	S	R	S	R	S	R	S	R	S	R
	20__		20__		20__		20__		20__	
Email	S	R	S	R	S	R	S	R	S	R

Section 3

Address	20__		20__		20__		20__		20__	
	S	R	S	R	S	R	S	R	S	R
	20__		20__		20__		20__		20__	
Email	S	R	S	R	S	R	S	R	S	R

Section 4

Address	20__		20__		20__		20__		20__	
	S	R	S	R	S	R	S	R	S	R
	20__		20__		20__		20__		20__	
Email	S	R	S	R	S	R	S	R	S	R

W

Name

Address

20__		20__		20__		20__		20__	
S	R	S	R	S	R	S	R	S	R

20__		20__		20__		20__		20__	
S	R	S	R	S	R	S	R	S	R

Email

Name

Address

20__		20__		20__		20__		20__	
S	R	S	R	S	R	S	R	S	R

20__		20__		20__		20__		20__	
S	R	S	R	S	R	S	R	S	R

Email

Name

Address

20__		20__		20__		20__		20__	
S	R	S	R	S	R	S	R	S	R

20__		20__		20__		20__		20__	
S	R	S	R	S	R	S	R	S	R

Email

Name

Address

20__		20__		20__		20__		20__	
S	R	S	R	S	R	S	R	S	R

20__		20__		20__		20__		20__	
S	R	S	R	S	R	S	R	S	R

Email

X

Name										

Address	20__		20__		20__		20__		20__	
	S	R	S	R	S	R	S	R	S	R
	20__		20__		20__		20__		20__	
Email	S	R	S	R	S	R	S	R	S	R

Name										

Address	20__		20__		20__		20__		20__	
	S	R	S	R	S	R	S	R	S	R
	20__		20__		20__		20__		20__	
Email	S	R	S	R	S	R	S	R	S	R

Name										

Address	20__		20__		20__		20__		20__	
	S	R	S	R	S	R	S	R	S	R
	20__		20__		20__		20__		20__	
Email	S	R	S	R	S	R	S	R	S	R

Name										

Address	20__		20__		20__		20__		20__	
	S	R	S	R	S	R	S	R	S	R
	20__		20__		20__		20__		20__	
Email	S	R	S	R	S	R	S	R	S	R

X

Name

Address	20__		20__		20__		20__		20__	
	S	R	S	R	S	R	S	R	S	R
	20__		20__		20__		20__		20__	
	S	R	S	R	S	R	S	R	S	R
Email										

Name

Address	20__		20__		20__		20__		20__	
	S	R	S	R	S	R	S	R	S	R
	20__		20__		20__		20__		20__	
	S	R	S	R	S	R	S	R	S	R
Email										

Name

Address	20__		20__		20__		20__		20__	
	S	R	S	R	S	R	S	R	S	R
	20__		20__		20__		20__		20__	
	S	R	S	R	S	R	S	R	S	R
Email										

Name

Address	20__		20__		20__		20__		20__	
	S	R	S	R	S	R	S	R	S	R
	20__		20__		20__		20__		20__	
	S	R	S	R	S	R	S	R	S	R
Email										

Name

Address	20__		20__		20__		20__		20__	
	S	R	S	R	S	R	S	R	S	R
	20__		20__		20__		20__		20__	
Email	S	R	S	R	S	R	S	R	S	R

Name

Address	20__		20__		20__		20__		20__	
	S	R	S	R	S	R	S	R	S	R
	20__		20__		20__		20__		20__	
Email	S	R	S	R	S	R	S	R	S	R

Name

Address	20__		20__		20__		20__		20__	
	S	R	S	R	S	R	S	R	S	R
	20__		20__		20__		20__		20__	
Email	S	R	S	R	S	R	S	R	S	R

Name

Address	20__		20__		20__		20__		20__	
	S	R	S	R	S	R	S	R	S	R
	20__		20__		20__		20__		20__	
Email	S	R	S	R	S	R	S	R	S	R

X

Name											
Address	20__		20__		20__		20__		20__	
	S	R	S	R	S	R	S	R	S	R
	20__		20__		20__		20__		20__	
Email	S	R	S	R	S	R	S	R	S	R

Name											
Address	20__		20__		20__		20__		20__	
	S	R	S	R	S	R	S	R	S	R
	20__		20__		20__		20__		20__	
Email	S	R	S	R	S	R	S	R	S	R

Name											
Address	20__		20__		20__		20__		20__	
	S	R	S	R	S	R	S	R	S	R
	20__		20__		20__		20__		20__	
Email	S	R	S	R	S	R	S	R	S	R

Name											
Address	20__		20__		20__		20__		20__	
	S	R	S	R	S	R	S	R	S	R
	20__		20__		20__		20__		20__	
Email	S	R	S	R	S	R	S	R	S	R

		X

Name

Address	20__		20__		20__		20__		20__	
	S	R	S	R	S	R	S	R	S	R
	20__		20__		20__		20__		20__	
Email	S	R	S	R	S	R	S	R	S	R

Name

Address	20__		20__		20__		20__		20__	
	S	R	S	R	S	R	S	R	S	R
	20__		20__		20__		20__		20__	
Email	S	R	S	R	S	R	S	R	S	R

Name

Address	20__		20__		20__		20__		20__	
	S	R	S	R	S	R	S	R	S	R
	20__		20__		20__		20__		20__	
Email	S	R	S	R	S	R	S	R	S	R

Name

Address	20__		20__		20__		20__		20__	
	S	R	S	R	S	R	S	R	S	R
	20__		20__		20__		20__		20__	
Email	S	R	S	R	S	R	S	R	S	R

X

Name

Address

20__		20__		20__		20__		20__	
S	R	S	R	S	R	S	R	S	R

20__		20__		20__		20__		20__	
S	R	S	R	S	R	S	R	S	R

Email

Name

Address

20__		20__		20__		20__		20__	
S	R	S	R	S	R	S	R	S	R

20__		20__		20__		20__		20__	
S	R	S	R	S	R	S	R	S	R

Email

Name

Address

20__		20__		20__		20__		20__	
S	R	S	R	S	R	S	R	S	R

20__		20__		20__		20__		20__	
S	R	S	R	S	R	S	R	S	R

Email

Name

Address

20__		20__		20__		20__		20__	
S	R	S	R	S	R	S	R	S	R

20__		20__		20__		20__		20__	
S	R	S	R	S	R	S	R	S	R

Email

Name

Address	20__		20__		20__		20__		20__	
	S	R	S	R	S	R	S	R	S	R
	20__		20__		20__		20__		20__	
Email	S	R	S	R	S	R	S	R	S	R

Name

Address	20__		20__		20__		20__		20__	
	S	R	S	R	S	R	S	R	S	R
	20__		20__		20__		20__		20__	
Email	S	R	S	R	S	R	S	R	S	R

Name

Address	20__		20__		20__		20__		20__	
	S	R	S	R	S	R	S	R	S	R
	20__		20__		20__		20__		20__	
Email	S	R	S	R	S	R	S	R	S	R

Name

Address	20__		20__		20__		20__		20__	
	S	R	S	R	S	R	S	R	S	R
	20__		20__		20__		20__		20__	
Email	S	R	S	R	S	R	S	R	S	R

Y

Name										

Entry 1

Address	20__		20__		20__		20__		20__	
	S	R	S	R	S	R	S	R	S	R
	20__		20__		20__		20__		20__	
Email	S	R	S	R	S	R	S	R	S	R

Entry 2

Name										

Address	20__		20__		20__		20__		20__	
	S	R	S	R	S	R	S	R	S	R
	20__		20__		20__		20__		20__	
Email	S	R	S	R	S	R	S	R	S	R

Entry 3

Name										

Address	20__		20__		20__		20__		20__	
	S	R	S	R	S	R	S	R	S	R
	20__		20__		20__		20__		20__	
Email	S	R	S	R	S	R	S	R	S	R

Entry 4

Name										

Address	20__		20__		20__		20__		20__	
	S	R	S	R	S	R	S	R	S	R
	20__		20__		20__		20__		20__	
Email	S	R	S	R	S	R	S	R	S	R

Name

Address

20__		20__		20__		20__		20__	
S	R	S	R	S	R	S	R	S	R

20__		20__		20__		20__		20__	
S	R	S	R	S	R	S	R	S	R

Email

Name

Address

20__		20__		20__		20__		20__	
S	R	S	R	S	R	S	R	S	R

20__		20__		20__		20__		20__	
S	R	S	R	S	R	S	R	S	R

Email

Name

Address

20__		20__		20__		20__		20__	
S	R	S	R	S	R	S	R	S	R

20__		20__		20__		20__		20__	
S	R	S	R	S	R	S	R	S	R

Email

Name

Address

20__		20__		20__		20__		20__	
S	R	S	R	S	R	S	R	S	R

20__		20__		20__		20__		20__	
S	R	S	R	S	R	S	R	S	R

Email

Y

Name										
Address	20__		20__		20__		20__		20__	
	S	R	S	R	S	R	S	R	S	R
	20__		20__		20__		20__		20__	
Email	S	R	S	R	S	R	S	R	S	R

Name										
Address	20__		20__		20__		20__		20__	
	S	R	S	R	S	R	S	R	S	R
	20__		20__		20__		20__		20__	
Email	S	R	S	R	S	R	S	R	S	R

Name										
Address	20__		20__		20__		20__		20__	
	S	R	S	R	S	R	S	R	S	R
	20__		20__		20__		20__		20__	
Email	S	R	S	R	S	R	S	R	S	R

Name										
Address	20__		20__		20__		20__		20__	
	S	R	S	R	S	R	S	R	S	R
	20__		20__		20__		20__		20__	
Email	S	R	S	R	S	R	S	R	S	R

	Y

Name

Address

	20__		20__		20__		20__		20__	
	S	R	S	R	S	R	S	R	S	R

	20__		20__		20__		20__		20__	
Email	S	R	S	R	S	R	S	R	S	R

Name

Address

	20__		20__		20__		20__		20__	
	S	R	S	R	S	R	S	R	S	R

	20__		20__		20__		20__		20__	
Email	S	R	S	R	S	R	S	R	S	R

Name

Address

	20__		20__		20__		20__		20__	
	S	R	S	R	S	R	S	R	S	R

	20__		20__		20__		20__		20__	
Email	S	R	S	R	S	R	S	R	S	R

Name

Address

	20__		20__		20__		20__		20__	
	S	R	S	R	S	R	S	R	S	R

	20__		20__		20__		20__		20__	
Email	S	R	S	R	S	R	S	R	S	R

Y

Name

Address	20__		20__		20__		20__		20__	
	S	R	S	R	S	R	S	R	S	R
	20__		20__		20__		20__		20__	
Email	S	R	S	R	S	R	S	R	S	R

Name

Address	20__		20__		20__		20__		20__	
	S	R	S	R	S	R	S	R	S	R
	20__		20__		20__		20__		20__	
Email	S	R	S	R	S	R	S	R	S	R

Name

Address	20__		20__		20__		20__		20__	
	S	R	S	R	S	R	S	R	S	R
	20__		20__		20__		20__		20__	
Email	S	R	S	R	S	R	S	R	S	R

Name

Address	20__		20__		20__		20__		20__	
	S	R	S	R	S	R	S	R	S	R
	20__		20__		20__		20__		20__	
Email	S	R	S	R	S	R	S	R	S	R

Name

Address	20__		20__		20__		20__		20__	
	S	R	S	R	S	R	S	R	S	R
	20__		20__		20__		20__		20__	
Email	S	R	S	R	S	R	S	R	S	R

Name

Address	20__		20__		20__		20__		20__	
	S	R	S	R	S	R	S	R	S	R
	20__		20__		20__		20__		20__	
Email	S	R	S	R	S	R	S	R	S	R

Name

Address	20__		20__		20__		20__		20__	
	S	R	S	R	S	R	S	R	S	R
	20__		20__		20__		20__		20__	
Email	S	R	S	R	S	R	S	R	S	R

Name

Address	20__		20__		20__		20__		20__	
	S	R	S	R	S	R	S	R	S	R
	20__		20__		20__		20__		20__	
Email	S	R	S	R	S	R	S	R	S	R

	Z

Name

Address	20__		20__		20__		20__		20__	
	S	R	S	R	S	R	S	R	S	R

	20__		20__		20__		20__		20__	
Email	S	R	S	R	S	R	S	R	S	R

Name

Address	20__		20__		20__		20__		20__	
	S	R	S	R	S	R	S	R	S	R

	20__		20__		20__		20__		20__	
Email	S	R	S	R	S	R	S	R	S	R

Name

Address	20__		20__		20__		20__		20__	
	S	R	S	R	S	R	S	R	S	R

	20__		20__		20__		20__		20__	
Email	S	R	S	R	S	R	S	R	S	R

Name

Address	20__		20__		20__		20__		20__	
	S	R	S	R	S	R	S	R	S	R

	20__		20__		20__		20__		20__	
Email	S	R	S	R	S	R	S	R	S	R

Name										

Address	20__		20__		20__		20__		20__	
	S	R	S	R	S	R	S	R	S	R
	20__		20__		20__		20__		20__	
Email	S	R	S	R	S	R	S	R	S	R

Name										

Address	20__		20__		20__		20__		20__	
	S	R	S	R	S	R	S	R	S	R
	20__		20__		20__		20__		20__	
Email	S	R	S	R	S	R	S	R	S	R

Name										

Address	20__		20__		20__		20__		20__	
	S	R	S	R	S	R	S	R	S	R
	20__		20__		20__		20__		20__	
Email	S	R	S	R	S	R	S	R	S	R

Name										

Address	20__		20__		20__		20__		20__	
	S	R	S	R	S	R	S	R	S	R
	20__		20__		20__		20__		20__	
Email	S	R	S	R	S	R	S	R	S	R

Z

Name

Address	20__		20__		20__		20__		20__	
	S	R	S	R	S	R	S	R	S	R
	20__		20__		20__		20__		20__	
Email	S	R	S	R	S	R	S	R	S	R

Name

Address	20__		20__		20__		20__		20__	
	S	R	S	R	S	R	S	R	S	R
	20__		20__		20__		20__		20__	
Email	S	R	S	R	S	R	S	R	S	R

Name

Address	20__		20__		20__		20__		20__	
	S	R	S	R	S	R	S	R	S	R
	20__		20__		20__		20__		20__	
Email	S	R	S	R	S	R	S	R	S	R

Name

Address	20__		20__		20__		20__		20__	
	S	R	S	R	S	R	S	R	S	R
	20__		20__		20__		20__		20__	
Email	S	R	S	R	S	R	S	R	S	R

Z

Name

Address	20__		20__		20__		20__		20__	
	S	R	S	R	S	R	S	R	S	R
	20__		20__		20__		20__		20__	
Email	S	R	S	R	S	R	S	R	S	R

Name

Address	20__		20__		20__		20__		20__	
	S	R	S	R	S	R	S	R	S	R
	20__		20__		20__		20__		20__	
Email	S	R	S	R	S	R	S	R	S	R

Name

Address	20__		20__		20__		20__		20__	
	S	R	S	R	S	R	S	R	S	R
	20__		20__		20__		20__		20__	
Email	S	R	S	R	S	R	S	R	S	R

Name

Address	20__		20__		20__		20__		20__	
	S	R	S	R	S	R	S	R	S	R
	20__		20__		20__		20__		20__	
Email	S	R	S	R	S	R	S	R	S	R

Z

Name										
Address	20__		20__		20__		20__		20__	
	S	R	S	R	S	R	S	R	S	R
	20__		20__		20__		20__		20__	
Email	S	R	S	R	S	R	S	R	S	R

Name										
Address	20__		20__		20__		20__		20__	
	S	R	S	R	S	R	S	R	S	R
	20__		20__		20__		20__		20__	
Email	S	R	S	R	S	R	S	R	S	R

Name										
Address	20__		20__		20__		20__		20__	
	S	R	S	R	S	R	S	R	S	R
	20__		20__		20__		20__		20__	
Email	S	R	S	R	S	R	S	R	S	R

Name										
Address	20__		20__		20__		20__		20__	
	S	R	S	R	S	R	S	R	S	R
	20__		20__		20__		20__		20__	
Email	S	R	S	R	S	R	S	R	S	R

Keep Track Books brings you
a variety of essential notebooks —
including Christmas card address books
with the same interior as this one,
but with different cover designs.

Search for 'Keep Track Books' on Amazon
or visit www.lusciousbooks.co.uk
to discover more notebooks.

Printed in Great Britain
by Amazon

54622271R00093